Boots

GUIDE TO

CAT CARE

Boots

GUIDE TO

CAT CARE

DAVID TAYLOR B.V.M.S., F.R.C.V.S.

Project editor Judith More
Art editor Carole Ash

Assistant designer Tina Vaughan
Assistant editor Janice Lacock

Senior art editor Peter Luff
Managing editor Alan Buckingham

Boots Guide to Cat Care was conceived, edited and designed by Dorling Kindersley Limited, 9 Henrietta Street, Covent Garden, London WC2E 8PS from material previously published in *You & Your Cat* by David Taylor

Published on behalf of The Boots company Plc Nottingham England by Dorling Kindersley Limited, 9 Henrietta Street, Covent Garden, London WC2E 8PS

ISBN 0 86318 210 0

Printed in Hong Kong by
Mandarin Offset Marketing (HK) Ltd

CONTENTS

INTRODUCTION

The human race can be divided into two categories: *ailurophiles* and *ailurophobes* – cat lovers and the underprivileged. The appreciation of cats is engraved deep in the human soul, and is of ancient origin. The first tamed cats were used for pest control in ancient Egypt, probably around 3,000 BC, and came to be loved as household companions and worshipped as gods. Since then, despite a change of fortune in the Middle Ages when they were persecuted by the Christian church, cats have become increasingly popular as pets. The reasons for their popularity are easy to see.

Cats are inexpensive to buy – you can obtain a non-pedigree from a friend or a humane society for nothing, and even a pedigree kitten from a breeder, with a few rare and expensive exceptions, will only cost the equivalent of a couple of days' pay for the average citizen. And cats cost very little to feed and care for compared to other popular pets such as dogs or ponies.

Although cheap to acquire and cheap to run, in pure monetary terms, a cat is worth its weight in gold to its new owner. It provides amusement and companionship, as well as adding a touch of style and elegance to your home. Cats will live happily in the smallest of flats, and because they don't require 24-hour attention are excellent pets for working owners. Elderly folk, too, benefit from their companionship, and young people can learn a lot by having a cat of their own to care for. The stewardship of a cat isn't difficult: it won't make the same exercise demands as a dog, and it doesn't require a battery of costly technical equipment, such as that required for aquarium fishes.

Unlike dogs, cats don't take lightly to being "owned". Their individuality is never up for grabs so for a good relationship with your cat, don't treat it as a possession; instead, try to see it as a sojourner in your household, choosing to spend its time with you and asking nothing in return apart from a modest supply of food and drink.

A cat's effection has to be won. Unlike a dog, it won't remain with a poor owner out of a misguided sense of loyalty. On the other hand, a cat will recognize an understanding, appreciative owner and respond with affection and respect. In order to get the best out of your feline friend, you must understand its nature and behave towards it accordingly. In particular, cats have a boundless sense of curiosity so you will need to safeguard your pet from potential dangers, just as a parent protects a child.

This book is divided into three sections: *Caring For Your Cat*, *Feeding* and *Health Care*. The first chapter introduces all the equipment you will need to care for your cat and shows you how to look after it. Grooming and handling techniques are explained as well as advice on travelling and training. The *Feeding* chapter gives invaluable information on providing a healthy diet for your pet, feeding methods, and suitable types of food. Finally, the *Health Care* chapter explains how to detect signs of ill-health in your cat, when you may treat an ailment at home and when you should seek veterinary advice, what action you should take if your cat has an accident, general advice on keeping your cat healthy and how to care for a sick animal.

Caring for a cat requires an understanding and appreciation of its basic nature. If you read the information and follow the advice given in this "owner's manual" you and your cat should enjoy a long and happy friendship.

Cats and children (above)
Children appreciate the amusement and affectionate contact that a cat provides. And under a parent's guidance, a child can learn to become a responsible pet owner.

1

CARING FOR YOUR CAT

Adding a cat to your household isn't just a matter of bringing one home. You will have to learn how to treat and care for your cat on a day-to-day basis — from picking it up correctly to transporting it safely. This may sound like a lot of work, but don't be alarmed. Cat care is basically a matter of commonsense, and won't take up too much of your time. Like you, the new member of the household will need its own "possessions" and equipment. This chapter covers the cat's bed, travelling container, door flap and pen, grooming and toilet training equipment.

Inspecting your prospective cat

Whatever kind of cat you are after, and no matter where you obtain it, there is one golden rule: always make a careful study of the cat's condition and state of health. *Never* take on a cat that is sick or not up to the mark, no matter how convincing the vendor's excuse may be. If your request to examine the cat is rejected, don't buy – any responsible vendor will realize it is reasonable to check a new pet thoroughly.

Before inspecting the animal, wash your hands thoroughly and play with the cat a little in order to put it at ease. Then grasp the body firmly but gently throughout the examination to prevent the cat from escaping. Take it slowly – any sudden movements may alarm the cat.

HOW TO EXAMINE A KITTEN

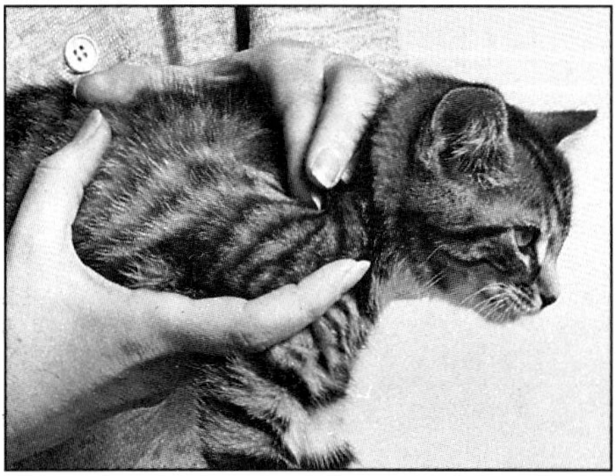

Coat
Feel the texture of the kitten's coat, which should be smooth and unmatted. And look for fleas or other pests.

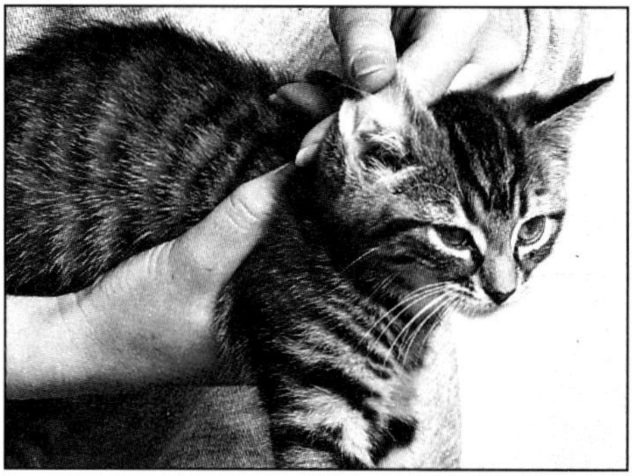

Ears
The kitten's ears should be clean and dry. Make sure they aren't filled with wax (see p. 57).

Eyes and nose
Check that the "haws" (third eyelids, see p. 55) don't protrude, the eyes are clean and bright, and the nose is damp.

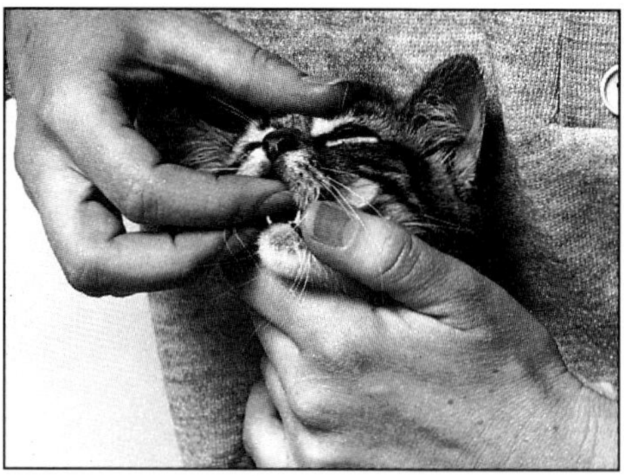

Mouth and teeth
A healthy kitten should have a pink mouth and white teeth. Check that the gums aren't inflamed.

WHAT SEX IS THE KITTEN?

Although sexing adult cats is fairly easy, differentiating between male and female kittens may not be. To do so, lift the tail and look at the opening beneath the anus. A female kitten can be distinguished by the closeness of her vulva to the anus, and the two openings may appear to be joined together. In the case of a male kitten, there is a raised dark area beneath the anus, which will develop into testicles, and below this, the penis.

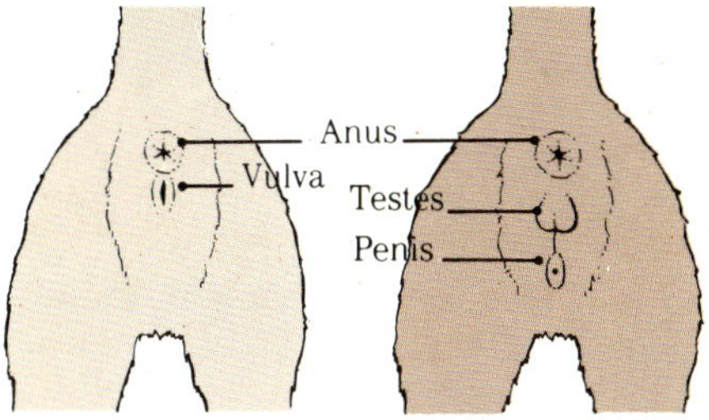

Female organs **Male organs**

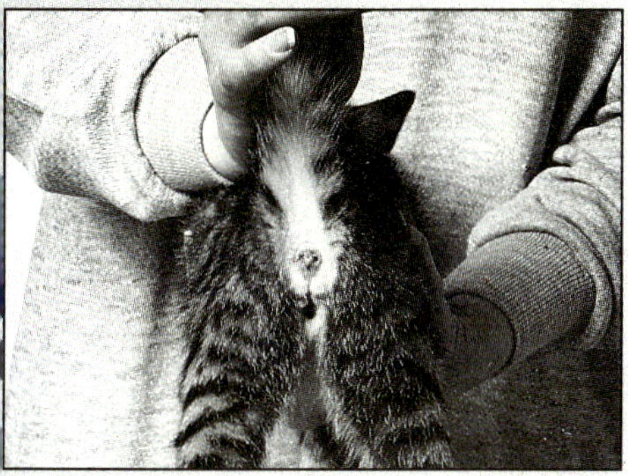

Anal area

Lift the kitten's tail and look for any signs of diarrhoea. The anal area should be clean.

Abdomen

Gently feel under the abdomen with one hand. It should be slightly rounded, but not hard. Make sure there are no lumps (a sign of a hernia). Then let the kitten move around freely so that you can see if it is lame.

Preparing for a new cat's arrival

Before you bring a new cat or kitten home, you should think carefully about potential hazards and move any dangerous objects out of its range. Remember that the inquisitive nature of cats can lead them into danger. In particular, keep washing machine, fridge and oven doors shut at all times, install a safety guard around an open fire, and always disconnect power when electric points are not in use.

Settling in

When you bring the cat home, allow it to explore its surroundings thoroughly on its own, introducing it to one room at a time, keeping other pets away. Then let them into the room where you are holding the newcomer, supervising the initial encounters carefully. In most cases any initial antipathy will gradually fade. Be careful not to neglect your old pets in favour of the new one.

Allowing the cat out of doors

In the first week, handle and fuss over the cat prior to any planned release into the garden. When the cat is eventually allowed outdoors, accompany it on its first few "sallies", and fit it with a collar bearing your name and address in case it gets lost. Young cats shouldn't be allowed outdoors in inclement weather, and no newly arrived cat, whatever its age, should be allowed to roam at night.

Vaccination and registration

All kittens should be vaccinated against Feline Enteritis and Feline Influenza (see pp.64 and 49) and receive regular "boosters" thereafter. Written veterinary certificates confirm that they have been given. If you have other cats and are anxious to keep them free from Feline Leukaemia (see p.79), ask a vet to carry out a blood test on the new cat.

If your kitten is a pedigree, it should be registered under an individual name, along with details of its colour and parents, when it is about five weeks old. Unless this is done, it won't be permitted to enter a cat show in a pedigree class.

Feline bedtime

Every cat should have its own sleeping place. This will give it a safe retreat, especially in times of illness or insecurity. However, many kittens prefer to spend the night in their owner's beds. If you object to this, start a night time routine by putting your cat in its own bed just before you retire. Switch off the light and shut the door. Don't forget to leave its litter tray and water bowl accessible. To start with, your kitten probably won't like this enforced segregation, but in a week or two it will settle down quietly each night.

You should clean your pet's bed and bedding regularly. Wash the bed by scrubbing it thoroughly with a non-toxic

SAFETY TIPS

- Don't leave sharp utensils out
- Don't leave toxic household products in accessible places
- Don't permit your cat to walk on kitchen surfaces, especially the hob
- Don't let your cat near when you are cooking with boiling liquids
- Don't leave polythene bags out – if a cat climbs inside it may suffocate
- Don't put a hot electric iron where your cat could knock into it
- Don't leave small objects where your cat may swallow or step on them
- Don't allow cats onto a high balcony

EQUIPMENT FOR A NEW CAT

Although pet shops sell a wide range of equipment for cats, few items are vital. Of the selection shown here, only the following are essential: a cat basket, litter tray and scoop, carrying basket, food and water dishes, grooming tools and a collar. Other items can be purchased as the kitten grows if you feel they are necessary.

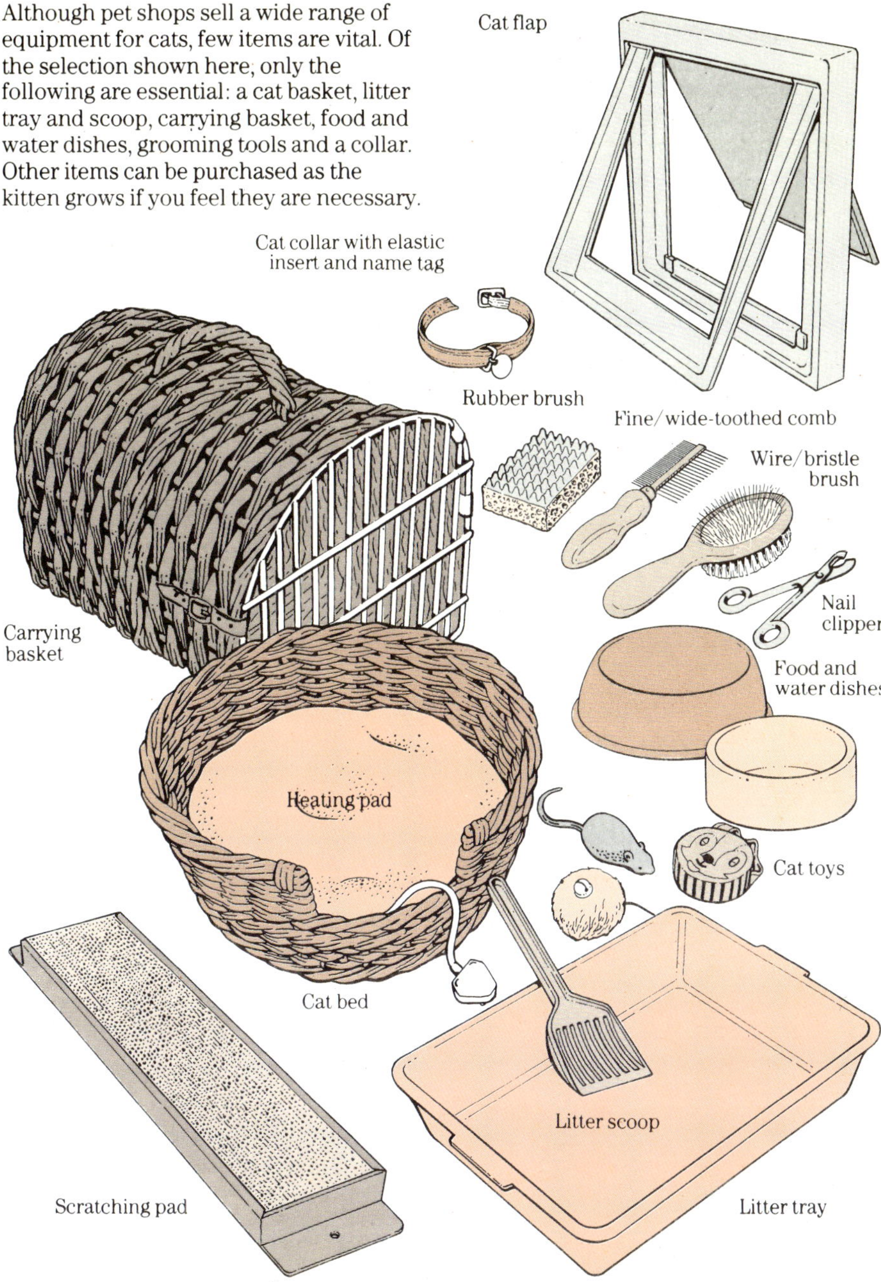

BASIC RULES FOR EVERY CAT OWNER

Feed your cat at regular times from its own bowl. Keep this dish separate from the family's crockery.

Give your cat its own bed – don't let it use yours.

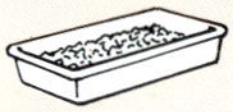

Clean the litter tray out daily.

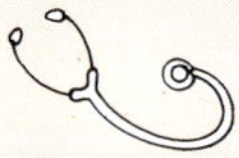

If you don't want your new kitten to be a mother or father, consult the vet about neutering it.

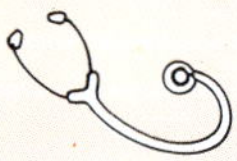

Register your cat with your chosen vet as a matter of routine (don't wait for an emergency).

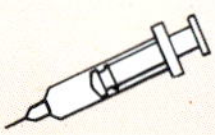

Make sure that your pet's "booster" vaccinations are kept up-to-date.

Groom your cat regularly – daily if it is a longhair – and check for the presence of fleas.

Establish behaviour rules early on – it is no good trying to stop a cat scratching the furniture after several years.

When you go on holiday, make arrangements for someone to look after your pet beforehand.

Keep your cat indoors during celebrations involving fireworks.

If you obtain a new cat or move home, never let your pet out until it has had time to adjust to its new environment.

If your queen is breeding, don't take the kittens from her until they are at least 6 weeks old.

disinfectant diluted in some hot water. Once the bed is dry, add a fresh layer of newspaper, then launder or replace the fabric bedding.

Leaving your cat unattended

A cat can be left alone in a house or flat for 24 hours as long as adequate food, water and a tray of cat litter are provided. But it is unwise to leave your cat for more than 24 hours without arranging for someone to visit and change the supplies. If you are going away, it is better to get a neighbour to call each morning than to send it to a cattery. The cat will be much happier and there is less risk of disease.

Cats and indoor plants

Some cats have a tendency to vandalize certain species of indoor plant because they love the aroma and texture of the plants. If you object to your cat's "gardening", spray your plants with an odour-free (to humans), cat-repellent aerosol. And if your cat hasn't access to a garden, provide it with a small seedbox planted with herbs and weeds.

Certain houseplants are poisonous to cats and should be kept out of reach of your pet. Your vet will advise you on which plants are dangerous.

BEFORE GOING OUT CHECK:

- A litter tray is available
- Adequate food is available
- Fresh water is available
- Any doors you want shut are shut
- There are no safety hazards

Travelling with your cat

Cats don't enjoy enforced journeys, but if you follow the advice given here, you can transport your pet without distressing it.

Choosing a carrier
A travelling basket must be large enough for your cat, well-ventilated, completely "cat-proof", and easy to clean and carry.

Cheap, disposable cardboard carriers will suffice for an occasional trip to the vet, but they aren't strong enough for long-distance travelling. For more frequent trips, and where public transport is involved, choose a vinyl "hold-all" carrier. If you show your cat regularly, you will need a fibreglass or polyethylene carrier. Traditional wicker carriers are attractive, but they are draughty and difficult to clean.

Putting your cat in its carrier
Before you put your cat in its carrier, let it use its litter tray. Encourage it into the basket with some dried food, or lift the cat into the carrier by supporting the hind legs and holding the scruff.

Moving house with a cat
When moving house, don't send the cat in the furniture van – put it in its carrier and take it in the car with you. At the new house you should shut all the doors before releasing your cat. Make sure it is fitted with a collar and tag giving your new address before you allow it out.

Travelling by car
If a car journey lasts for more than half-an-hour, you should stop at reasonable intervals to allow your cat to use the litter tray and to eat and drink. Keep all the doors and windows closed when you stop, as the cat may try to escape.

Some owners allow their cat to travel loose, but this isn't advisable, and if your cat isn't used to travelling, you must restrict it to a carrier. In Britain it is an offence to have a loose cat in a car if the driver is the only occupant.

Travelling abroad and rabies
Your first priority is to investigate the quarantine regulations in the countries you are travelling to and from.

Britain is one of the world's few rabies-free countries, and remains so by imposing very strict quarantine laws. When you bring a cat into the U.K. from abroad, it will be quarantined for a period of six months, and during this time it will be given two anti-rabies inoculations. Likewise, a short quarantine period and/or an inoculation will be required if you take a cat from Britain to another controlled country.

Travelling by air or rail
If you ship your cat by air, you must contain it securely in a basket or box which complies with the regulations laid down by the airlines through the International Air Transport Association. In addition, some airlines add their own rules, so check this before you travel.

It is recommended that you give a light meal and a short drink two hours before dispatch. If the animal is nervous, you can give it a tranquilizer (prescribed by the vet) shortly before you deliver it to the airline's office.

ITEMS YOU SHOULD PACK:

- Litter tray
- Food
- Water
- Feeding dishes
- Blanket
- Toy
- Carrier

Handling techniques

It is almost impossible to resist handling a cat. And if they are handled correctly, most cats adore being picked up and cuddled. For a cat to enjoy being picked up it must feel comfortable and secure, and trust you completely. A cat's body must always be supported; if you pick it up incorrectly, with your hands under its arms and the rest of its body dangling in mid-air, a tolerant cat will wag its tail to show its displeasure, but a less placid animal will probably struggle, or even bite, to get free.

Correct handling is particularly important with new kittens, as their small rib cages are very fragile and can be bruised easily. And a sick cat will also need special handling; this method is covered in the chapter on *Health Care* (see pp. 86-7).

How often can I pick my cat up?
The number of times you handle your cat will depend on its temperament and on the treatment you want it to get used to. If you intend to show your pet you should get it used to being held up high at arm's length as a judge would when examining it. It is also a good idea to ask any visitors to make a point of handling it as this will help it to grow accustomed to the attentions of strangers.

Children and cats
It is very important that children are taught how to handle cats correctly, so that they always support the body firmly. If a child picks up a cat incorrectly it will scratch or bite in order to be freed.

Cradling a cat
Although humans like to hold a cat like a baby, tummy facing upwards and face looking into theirs, not all cats enjoy this. If your cat objects, don't insist on carrying it in this manner.

HOW TO PICK UP AND HOLD A CAT

Grown cats can be picked up with one hand around the stomach, just behind the front paws, and the other under the hind quarters. Once picked up, a cat will probably be happiest sitting in the crook of your arm, with its forepaws either leaning against your shoulder or held in your other hand. Your arms should be taking most of the cat's weight, and it should be sitting upright.

Don't pick up a kitten by the scruff of the neck as a mother cat would. Instead place one hand around its stomach and the other hand under its hind legs. A kitten should be small enough to sit on your palm as long as you have your other hand around its neck to support the head.

1 To pick up a cat without hurting it, place one hand under its front legs, and scoop it up by pushing your other hand under its hind quarters.

2 Bring the cat up level with your chest, all the time keeping one hand firmly under its hind quarters in order to support its full weight.

3 Lean the cat against you, using both arms and hands to support it.

Using your arm Often, the crook of your arm will make a useful support.

Supporting the body To hold a cat securely, put one hand round its upper chest near its neck.

Holding the hind quarters Support the cat by placing one hand under the cat's back legs.

Training your cat

As a cat owner you will need to spend some time training the animal to behave in an acceptable fashion. The best way to train it is to establish a routine right from the beginning of its life. Toilet training in particular must begin then. Wherever possible, feeding and grooming should be carried out at regular times of the day.

Toilet training

When a kitten first begins to eat solids at three or four weeks of age the time has come to introduce it to toilet training. Place the cat litter tray in a convenient, easily reached but quiet spot and put the kitten in it frequently, particularly when it looks ready to urinate or defecate, or indeed has begun to do so. You can tell if your kitten is about to urinate or defecate as it will crouch with its tail raised. *Never* rub the kitten's nose in its urine or droppings when it relieves itself in the wrong place, or, attracted by the scent, it will regard that area as its permanent "toilet". Always clean these areas scrupulously to avoid repetition of the soiling.

Responding to your call

All cats should be taught to respond to their own name – many have been rescued because they have called out in response to their owner's voice when trapped or in danger. If you use its name regularly, your cat will respond without difficulty, particularly at feeding time.

Using a cat flap

Another useful skill is the ability to use a cat flap. Your cat will probably hesitate

LEARNING TO USE A LITTER TRAY

As cats are very clean animals by nature, toilet training is relatively simple (see above), especially where a kitten has been brought up by its natural mother. With fostered kittens, their natural instinct to cover their faeces means that most will readily adopt the litter tray. However, if your kitten won't use it, check that the tray is in a quiet place where the kitten isn't being disturbed, and that the litter is fresh. Alternatively, it may be that your pet doesn't like the odour of the litter you are providing.

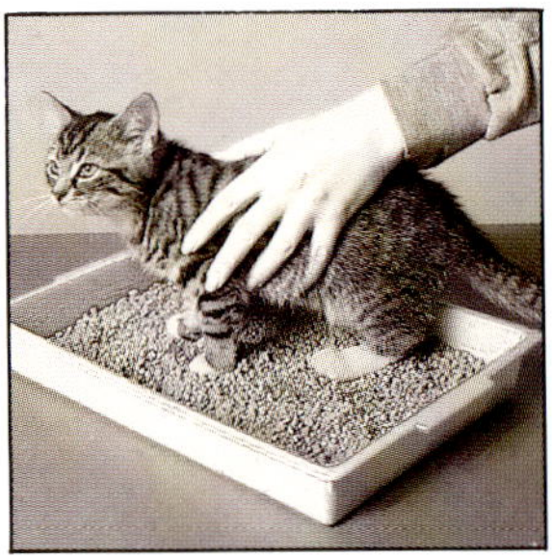

The basic litter tray
A simple tray filled with litter is the most usual form of toilet for cats. If you have more than one kitten, make sure it is big enough for them all to use.

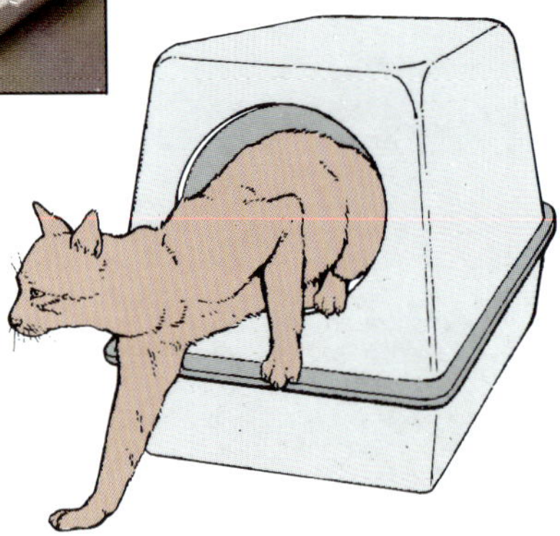

The "superloo"
A covered tray is ideal for nervous cats or those who like privacy.

to do so at first, because of the fear of being trapped, but it shouldn't be difficult to train it.

The cat door should be set no higher than six cms from the base of the door so that your cat can step rather than jump through it. Begin training by fastening the flap open and allowing your cat to investigate it. If you place some food on the other side this may tempt the cat through, but make sure that the flap is firmly fastened and won't drop down and alarm the cat. Once your pet has stepped through, release the flap and use a titbit to encourage it to step back, but this time help it to push the flap open.

The cat door
Once a cat has learnt to use a flap, it will enjoy the freedom it provides.

Coping with anti-social behaviour

Your cat may also need some "negative" training, for example to dissuade it from biting or jumping on people. The most effective way to do this is to say a firm "No" from kittenhood. It is not a good idea to chase the cat away as this may encourage it to think you are playing.

Scratching the furniture is less likely to be a problem if you allow your cat outdoors. It can then file its nails on rough wooden fencing or the bark of tree trunks. For a housebound cat, introduce a scratching post (see below).

Teaching tricks

Some owners like to teach their cats tricks such as begging for food. This can be done by rewarding with titbits or stroking. However, unlike a dog, a cat will only "perform" if it wants to, and no amount of training will make it do something that it doesn't want to do.

DISSUADING YOUR CAT FROM SCRATCHING

If your cat scratches your furniture in order to file its nails, grab it by the scruff and thrust it firmly at an alternative object. The "scratching post" must be stable enough to take the cat's weight.

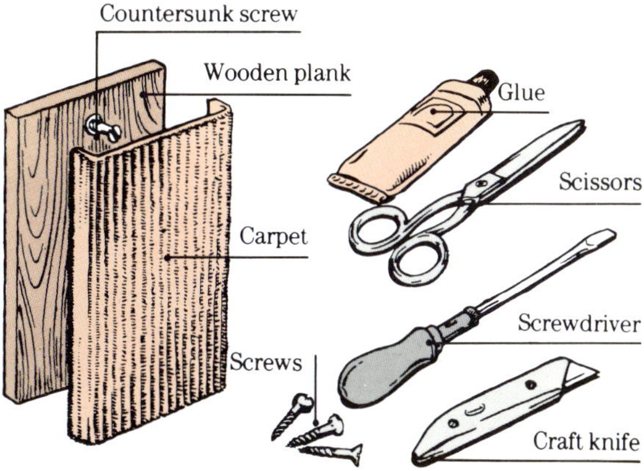

Making a scratching post
Screw a 30—60 cms long piece of wood planking to the wall in an unobtrusive corner of the room. Then glue your chosen material — hessian, carpet or bark — to the wood upright.

Basic grooming techniques

The best place to groom your cat, if the weather allows, is out of doors. Before you begin brushing and combing your cat you should check its ears, eyes, mouth and claws for any signs of potential health problems. Examine the inside of the inner ear flap for dirt, and clean it out with a piece of cotton wool dipped in olive oil. Examine your cat's teeth for tartar. Ideally, you should clean its teeth once a week (see p.60).

It is important to groom the coat regularly to prevent the cat ingesting accumulations of loose hair, known as "hairballs". These can become "glued" together in the cat's stomach and upset the digestive functions by obstructing the bowel (see p. 61).

CARE OF THE EYES

Your cat's eyes should be bright and clear, without any inflammation or discharge (see p. 51).

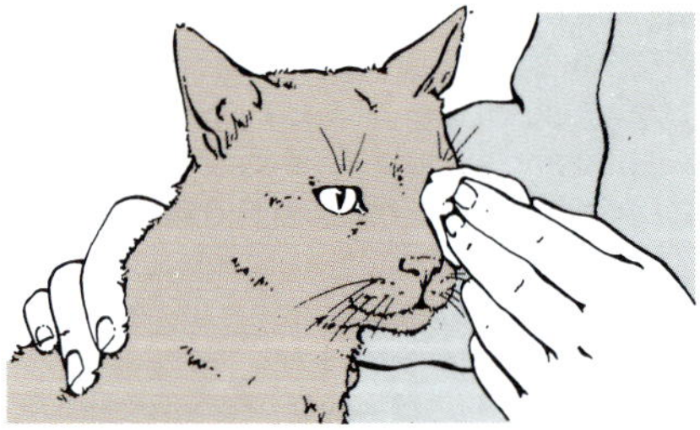

Cleaning the eyes
To clean a cat's eyes moisten a cotton wad in warm water and gently wipe the dirt away.

CARE OF THE CLAWS

A healthy, active cat's claws are trimmed automatically because they are worn down as it exercises. However, if your cat is old, or confined indoors, you should check its claws regularly as they may need trimming. Untrimmed claws may grow into the pad of the paw, and the cat will then need veterinary attention.

Trimming claws

If you need to cut a cat's claws, hold the animal firmly in your lap and press the pad of its paw with your fingers to make the claws come forward. Examine the claw carefully – the main part includes the pinkish-coloured quick which contains nerves. You must *not* cut this. The white tips are dead tissue, and cutting them won't hurt the cat.

Cleaning claws

Cat's claws don't often become caked with dirt, but if they do, you can clean them quite easily using damp cotton wool.

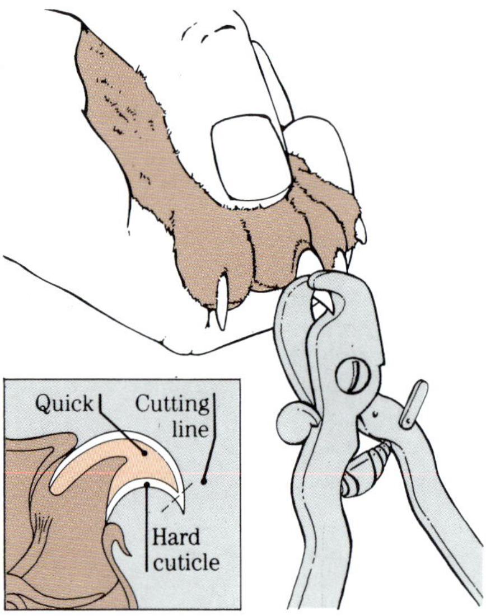

Cutting claws
Using very sharp scissors or special clippers, cut off the white tip. Make sure that you don't cut the quick.

BATHING A CAT

The kitchen sink will probably make the best "bath". Before you start, make sure that all the doors and windows are closed, and that the room is free from cold draughts. Place a rubber mat in the sink to stop the cat slipping.

If you think that your cat is going to struggle, put it in a cotton sack, leaving only its head visible. Pour the shampoo into the sack and lower the cat and sack into the water. You can then massage the cat through the sack and form a lather.

1 Fill the sink with about 5–10 cms of warm water. The water temperature should be as close to your cat's blood heat of 38.6°C as possible. To lift the cat in put one hand under its hind quarters, and hold the scruff of its neck with the other. If your cat prefers, allow it to rest its front paws out of the water.

2 Using a sponge, wet the cat's fur all over, except for its face. Next, rub a non-toxic cat or baby shampoo into the coat to produce a lather. Once the fur is full of soapy lather, rinse it thoroughly with warm water until there is no trace of soap in the rinse water. You will find that a spray attachment is the most efficient tool for this.

3 Lift the cat out of the sink and wrap it in a large, warm towel. Now you can wash its face with cotton wool dipped in warm water. Until the cat is totally dry you must keep it in a warm place. If it isn't afraid of hairdryers, you can use one on a low setting, taking care not to singe the coat. Once the fur is dry, comb it gently.

Grooming a longhaired cat

In the wild, a longhaired cat would moult in the winter only, but because domestic cats are kept in artificially lit and heated conditions, they moult all year round. As a result, longhaired cats need daily grooming – two 15–30 minute sessions – otherwise their coats will mat. If the matted balls of fur aren't dealt with at an early stage they will become painful, and you will have to get a vet to shave them off while the cat is anaesthetized. This isn't just painful for the cat – your pocket will be hurt too!

Before you start a grooming session take the opportunity to check your cat's ears, eyes, mouth and claws for cleanliness and signs of health problems (see p. 20).

GROOMING METHOD

1 With a wide-toothed comb, remove debris and tease out mats. Once this comb runs through the hair easily, change to a fine-toothed type.

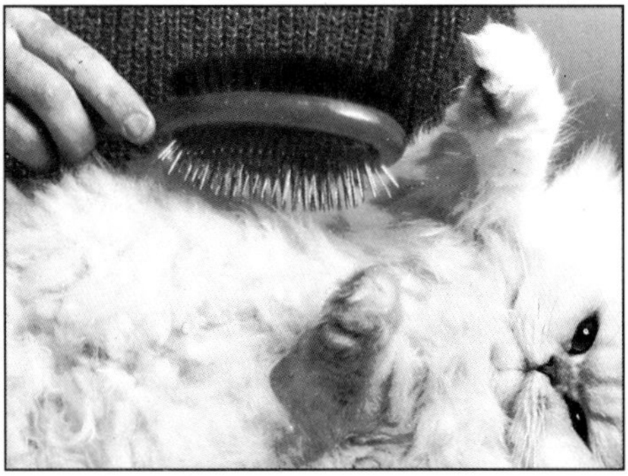

2 Using a wire brush, remove all dead hair. Pay particular attention to the rump, where you will probably be able to brush it out by the handful.

3 Brush some talcum powder or fuller's earth into the coat. This adds body and helps to separate the hairs. Brush out the powder immediately.

4 Run the fine-toothed comb through the hair in an upwards movement, brushing the fur out around the neck so that it forms a ruff.

GROOMING EQUIPMENT

You will need a wide and fine-toothed comb, a bristle and wire brush for the coat, and a toothbrush. You should also have blunt-ended scissors to cut mats, and bay rum conditioner (dark cats) or talc (light cats) to rub into the fur. And for a show cat use a slicker brush on the tail.

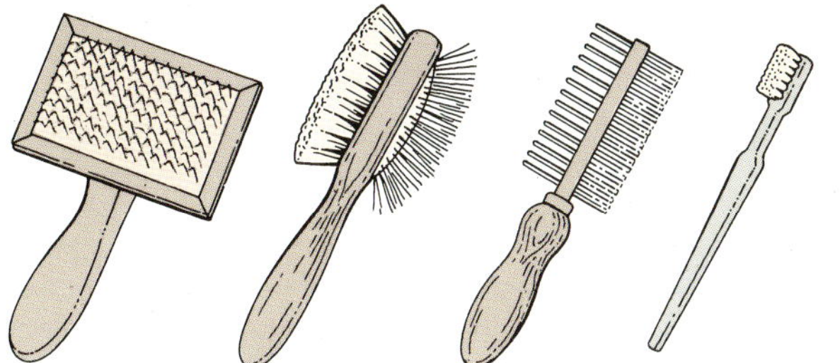

Slicker brush · Wire and bristle brush · Fine/wide-toothed comb · Toothbrush for cleaning face

5 With a toothbrush, gently brush the shorter hairs on the cat's face. Be careful not to get too close to its eyes.

6 Finally, repeat Step 4 with the wide-toothed comb, to separate the hair and help it to stand up. For show cats, use a slicker brush to fluff out the tail.

Grooming a shorthaired cat

A shorthaired cat doesn't need daily grooming as its coat is much easier to manage than that of a longhaired type. Moreover, shorthaired cats have longer tongues than their longhaired cousins, and so are efficient self-groomers. Two half-hour grooming sessions a week are therefore ample.

In fact, some people believe that if you groom a shorthaired cat more than twice a week it may stop grooming itself altogether. If you are an eager cat beautician and this news disappoints you, don't despair. There is a way in which you can indulge your love of grooming – you can spend some time every day conditioning the coat by stroking it along the lie of the hair.

GROOMING METHOD

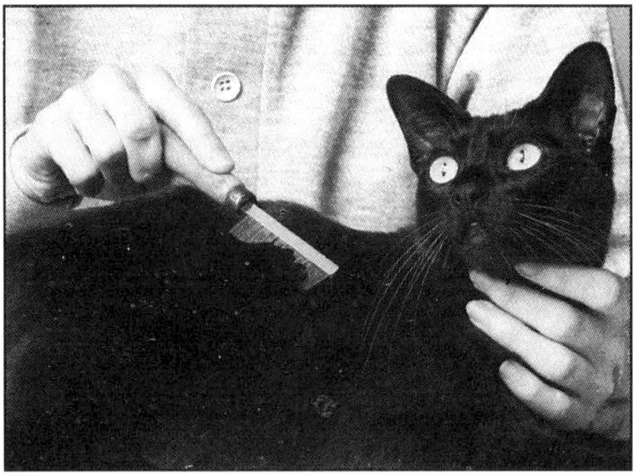

1 With a fine-toothed metal comb, work down the cat from its head to its tail. As you comb, look for black, shiny specks – a sign of fleas (see p. 83).

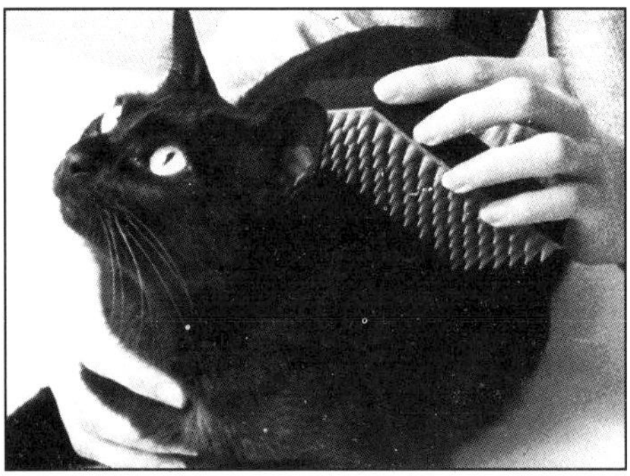

2 Use a rubber brush to brush along the lie of the hair. If your cat is Rex-coated, this brush is essential as it won't scratch the skin.

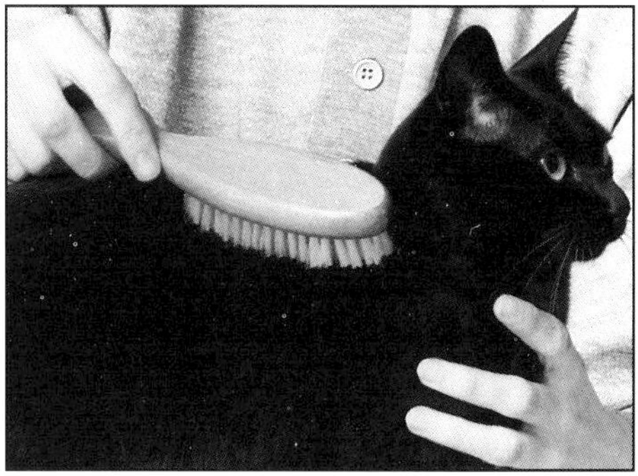

3 With some shorthairs you may prefer to use a soft natural bristle brush, rather than the rubber type. Again, work along the lie of the hair.

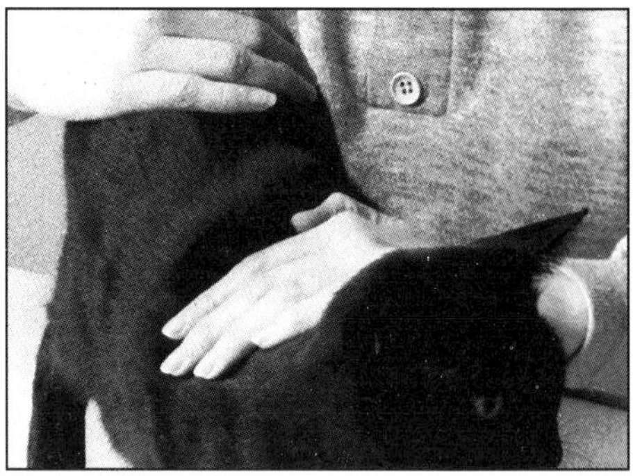

4 After brushing and combing, rub in some bay rum conditioner. This removes grease from the coat and brings out the brilliance of its colour.

GROOMING EQUIPMENT

You will need a fine-toothed metal comb, and a soft natural bristle or rubber brush. You should also have some bay rum conditioner to rub into the fur (suits all coat colours), and a velvet, silk or chamois leather cloth to polish the coat.

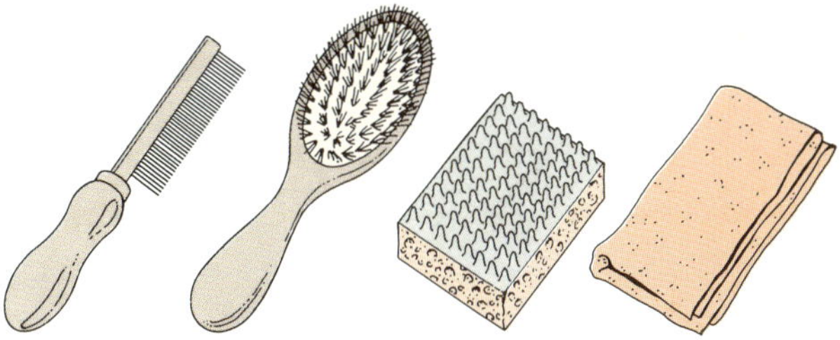

Fine-toothed comb | Soft natural bristle brush | Rubber brush | Chamois cloth

5 Finally, to bring up the glossy quality of a shorthaired cat's coat, especially just before a show, "polish" it with a piece of silk or velvet or a chamois leather cloth. Between grooming sessions you can keep up the shine by gently stroking the cat with a clean hand along the lie of the hair.

2

FEEDING

A correctly brought-up cat isn't very faddy, although it is often fussier than many humans are about freshness and hygiene in the kitchen. Don't make the mistake of turning your cat into a spoilt and unhealthy pet by feeding it continuously on its "favourite" brand of pet food; to keep it fit and well, you should give it a varied, well-balanced diet as described in this chapter.

Providing a healthy diet

Most of the dietary constituents that are essential to human life are just as important for a cat's well-being. However, they are needed and used in different proportions. Unlike us, the cat is a true carnivore, equipped to survive on a diet of other animals. When a cat eats its prey it consumes not just the muscle meat, but also the skin, bones and internal organs. This total diet contains almost everything that a cat needs to survive, and in the correct proportions.

Proteins

Found in meat, fish, eggs and cheese, proteins provide the amino acids that are the essential building blocks of body tissue, and are therefore vital for growth and repair. In the cat, proteins are also a source of energy calories. After being processed by the cat's body during digestion, proteins produce a considerable quantity of waste products. As a result, the kidneys have to be able to work hard to remove them from the body (see p. 33). To survive, a growing cat needs a minimum of about ten percent protein in its diet, and an adult cat requires six percent. However, a good feline diet should contain much more protein than that – between 25 and 30 percent should keep your cat strong and healthy.

Fats

A key source of calories for a cat, fats should form 15–40 percent of your pet's ration. The advantage of fats is that they don't load the kidneys with waste products, and therefore the fat content of your cat's diet should be increased as it gets older. Make sure that you don't feed fats that are old or rancid – although a hungry cat may accept such food, it can make it ill.

Carbohydrates

Another source of energy calories, carbohydrates are found in starchy food such as bread or potatoes. Although they aren't essential to a cat, if you want to include them in your pet's menu you can give up to 50 percent of its diet in this form. This type of food is also a useful source of the bulk (fibre) needed for a healthy bowel.

Minerals

As in humans, minerals of all kinds are essential for a cat's growth, and the maintenance of its body structures and vital functions. If you feed your cat a well-composed, varied diet, mineral deficiencies are most unlikely to occur.

Vitamins

Eating the complete prey animal, together with exposure to sunlight, provides wild cats with all the vitamins that they need. The domestic cat gets all its requirements either from a properly composed, broad diet, or from the supplements which are added to manufactured cat food. Unlike us, the cat doesn't need the vitamins B12, C and K in its diet. B12 is unneccessary to it, and C and K are synthesized within its body.

Choosing the right foods

Variety should be the spice of life when it comes to a cat's meals, so it is impossible to lay down a fixed diet sheet. Many different foods can be fed to a cat; the chart on the opposite page gives the advantages and disadvantages of the major types. When feeding your cat, you should ring the changes frequently, using all the foods mentioned in the chart. A useful guide is to give two parts by weight of a selection from the protein foods to one part of a selection of the fillers.

THE MAJOR FOODS

Type	Preparation	Value	Comments
PROTEIN **Manufactured** – dried, soft-moist and canned	● Ready-to-serve, no cooking involved	Formulated to provide a balanced diet	Convenient to use
Meat – beef, lamb or pork	● Bake or grill, then cut into small cubes	High in protein	Don't buy from knacker's yard. If you must boil it, use water as gravy on dried food
Offal	● Must always be cooked	High in protein	Don't buy from knacker's yard
Poultry and rabbit	● Feed cooked scraps	High in protein	Don't feed bones
Egg	● Serve whole, cooked and chopped ● Raw, separated yolks can be fed	Good source of protein	Don't feed raw egg whites. Don't give more than two whole eggs a week
Milk	● Pour it from the bottle!	Good source of protein and calcium	Gives some cats upset stomachs
Cheese	● Serve raw and grated ● Can be cooked with other foods	Excellent source of protein	
Fish	● Serve fresh and raw, steamed or grilled. If larger than a herring, chop and bone it ● Tinned fish in tomato or oil can be given	High in protein. Oily fish helps to dispel fur balls from the stomach	A diet of nothing but fish is unbalanced
FILLERS **Vegetables**	● Add cooked to meat or fish	Provides bulk and vitamins	No more than one-third of meal
Starchy foods	● Mix crumbled toast, pasta or potato with gravy or fish stock ● Cereal can be used with milk	Provides bulk	No more than one-third of meal
Fruit	● Occasional slices or segments	Source of vitamins	An occasional "treat" food

Feeding methods

Cats are "fussy" eaters: they like to eat fresh food little and often, out of clean bowls, and in a place that is free from noise, strong light or bustle.

Where to feed your cat

You should serve your pet's meals somewhere out of the general flow of traffic in the house, for example in a corner of the kitchen. Ideally, the cat should have a regular feeding area where it can eat in peace, and where the floor is impervious and easy to clean. Put a tray, mat or newspaper underneath the bowls to catch spills. If possible, avoid feeding your cat outdoors as meals spoil more readily in the open air, and there is also a risk of attracting rodents.

Bad feeding habits
Cats should be discouraged from foraging for food in dustbins or other unhealthy sites.

FEEDING EQUIPMENT

You will need three heavy plastic or glazed pottery bowls: one for food, one for water, and one for milk. And each cat should have its own set. Wash up a pet's dishes after each meal, keeping them separate from family ones.

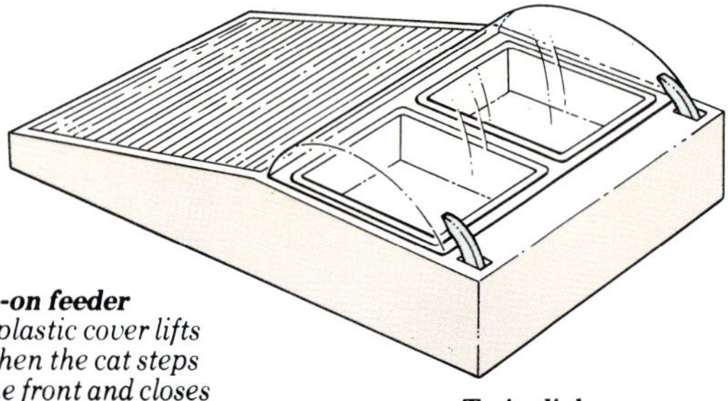

Step-on feeder
The plastic cover lifts up when the cat steps on the front and closes when it steps off, keeping food fresh all day.

Single bowls
Choose a sturdy bowl with a rim so that the cat can't tip it over easily.

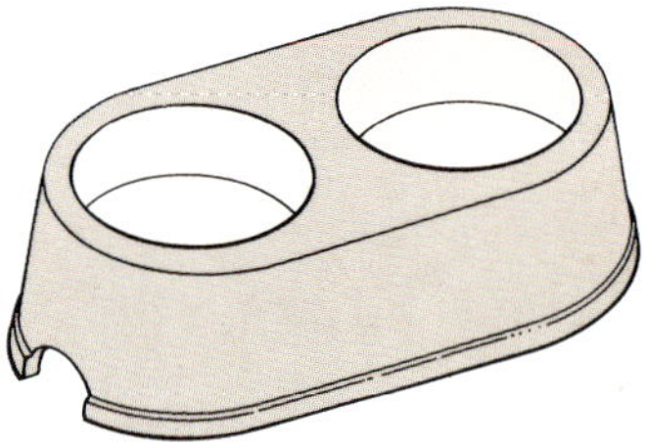

Twin dish
This design allows you to feed dried food and water side-by-side.

How much food should you provide?
Scientists have calculated that the daily requirement of a cat on a diet that contains 25 percent protein is 14 g of food per 450 g of body weight. The table below gives the total daily serving of food that a cat requires at different stages in its life. However, this is theoretical. In practice, like humans, cats' appetites vary widely – so use it as a guideline only.

Unlike dogs or humans, obese cats don't generally have health problems. It may be necessary to watch the outlines of show cats, but the ordinary fireside pet doesn't need to slim.

How often should you feed a cat?
Use the table below to assess how many meals a day your cat should have at each age of its life. Because fresh food and water is a "must" for cats, the main rule for feeding a cat is to give small amounts frequently. This will avoid waste, as a cat has the nose of an Egon Ronay inspector, and will stalk away from any dish that seems stale.

Coping with loss of appetite
A cat that has lost its appetite isn't necessarily ill. It may have been upset by travelling, or be feeling the effects of hot, humid weather. And queens on heat sometimes forget about their food until they "cool down". Another reason for a cat rejecting food may be that it has spoilt, as meat or fish that is slightly "off" produces chemicals that a highly sensitive feline nose can detect immediately. If none of these explanations fits, consider whether your pet may be dividing its culinary affections between you and the little old lady down the street who does a good line in cooked chicken livers. Duplicitous gourmandizing is far from uncommon, and can lead to an apparent disinterest in the food you provide, particularly if all you have to offer is the same old food.

However, if your pet rejects fresh food for more than half a day, and you are certain that none of the explanations given apply, it may well be unwell (see p. 59). If your cat has refused food for more than 24 hours, you should take it to the vet.

PLANNING YOUR CAT'S MEALS

Age	Meals per day	Amount in grams
KITTENS		
Weaning – 3 months	4–6	80–190
4–5 months	4–5	275
6–7 months	3–4	370
7–8 months	3	370
ADULTS		
Over 9 months	2–3	400
Pregnant queens	3–5	420–60
Senior citizens	3–6	300–70

DIET DON'TS

- Don't feed knacker's meat – it may be teeming with bacteria
- Don't feed poultry bones as these are small and splintery, and could choke a cat
- Don't give raw egg white – this contains a chemical called avidin that neutralizes biotin (an essential vitamin), making it unavailable to the cat
- Don't give a cat more than two eggs a week
- Don't boil fish – you will destroy the nutriments
- Don't feed dried food to a cat with bladder problems
- Don't give a cat proprietary dog food – the meat (protein) content isn't high enough

Food types

To give your cat a balanced diet it is important that you provide a varied selection of food. This can be provided by both fresh and pre-packed foods.

Pre-packed foods

There are three main kinds of pre-packed food marketed for cats: canned meat, soft-moist products and dried foods. All three types are convenient to use. However, such food can be very dull as the sole item on the menu. To provide variety in your cat's diet, alternate different brands and flavours.

Canned foods usually contain meat, fish salts, jellying agents, vitamins, colouring chemicals, water and, sometimes cereals. Most recipes are based on fish, chicken, beef, rabbit or offal. They contain 25-30 percent protein, and can therefore be used as a large component of a cat's rations. Cans are sterile and easy to store.

Dried mini-biscuits and granules contain cereals, fish, meat, yeast, vitamins, fat and colouring. They are cheaper than canned or soft-moist food, and are easy to store. Dried foods are not intended as a complete diet, but they can form an enjoyable part of your cat's intake. When you feed your cat on dried food, you *must* make sure that fresh water is always available to avoid causing bladder problems (see p.71).

Soft-moist pellets contain meat, soya beans, fats, vitamins, preservatives, colouring chemicals and, often, thickening agents and sugar. Though they are called "moist", some are positively wet – containing more than 33 percent water. Soft-moist foods can be used as a large part of a cat's diet as they usually contain just over 25 percent protein. Packed in foil sachets, they can be stored, but not as long as cans.

Fresh foods

If you feed mostly tinned food, you may like to give your cat a once- or twice-weekly meal of any of the fresh foods in the chart on p.29. This will provide some variety which your cat may enjoy as a change to its usual diet. If you do cook specially for your cat, season the food with iodized salt. This trace element is particularly important for pregnant queens, as it prevents re-absorption of the foetuses within the womb.

All cats are carnivores, and must have meat to survive. To avoid Toxoplasmosis (see p.67), all meats should be cooked. You should either mince or chop the food finely, or serve it in large lumps that can be torn up, since cats are unable to chew. If you give your cat chicken avoid any risk of its choking by making sure that you have removed all the bones.

Don't be alarmed if your pet insists on chewing grass or weeds. Grass is good for cats: it contains certain vitamins, and acts as an efficient emetic, helping the animal to regurgitate unwanted matter such as furballs. However, if your cat often grazes on your lawn, make sure that any fertilizer you use is non-toxic to avoid any risk of poisoning.

Supplements

If your cat is in good health, and you feed it a broad, varied diet, it shouldn't need extra vitamin or mineral supplements. If you do give them, they will simply be excreted. However, supplements are sometimes beneficial to sick animals; for example, iron tablets help an anaemic cat to recover. Such treatment should only be given on a vet's advice. Supplements are also useful for pregnant and nursing queens. Your vet will advise you on what types to give when necessary.

Liquids

Liquids are essential to feline health, although a cat can survive with a lower fluid intake than us in proportion to its body size.

Water

Although this isn't strictly a food, it is a necessary part of a cat's diet. Meat diets should contain high levels of water as well as of protein. An animal on a rich protein diet will produce plenty of urea, and therefore will need a good volume of water to flush this waste product away via the kidneys. So do cats need a larger quantity of water for their size than we do? In fact, they need less, because they are able to produce a far higher concentration of urea in their urine than we can (almost three times as strong), and this helps them to conserve water. And cats lose very little water through panting or sweating, and an insignificant quantity evaporates during breathing. Even big cats like lions have been recorded as going without a drink for up to 10 days.

Diets that contain cooked fish, tripe and certain tinned foods should give a creature the size of a cat much of the water that it needs. Moreover, cats get a large proportion of their daily water requirements by chemical action. The fats and carbohydrates in their food are "burnt" within their bodies and produce water molecules.

As long as fresh, clean water is always available, don't worry about how little of the stuff your pet seems to be drinking, unless you have settled for the lazy owner's diet of nothing but dried food pellets – in which case, an adequate intake of water is important to prevent urinary problems (see p. 71). Some cats don't drink at all in their owner's presence, but probably tipple at a puddle, or, like mine, imbibe bath water.

Lapping
A cat transfers liquid into its mouth by collecting it in its long tongue, which it curls into a spoon shape for the purpose.

Milk

Not strictly a liquid, milk is actually a food. Its prime value is as a source of calcium and phosphorus – a 200 ml serving will provide an adult cat's daily needs. However, some cats can't tolerate cow's milk, and get diarrhoea after drinking it (see p. 64). If your cat has a milk sensitivity, it may need supplements.

Alcohol

Unfortunately, some cats do fall victim to this human vice. Jack, a black tom from Brooklyn, was said to have given up drinking water at the tender age of three, preferring milk laced with Pernod. As he grew older, he demanded stiffer and stiffer saucers of "milk", until it was a question of lacing the Pernod lightly with milk. Jack gave up the ghost when he was eight years old, and, not surprisingly, a post-mortem found his liver in a sorry state. It isn't wise to give a cat alcohol, however small the quantity. The cat's body has no use for this poison, and may well be harmed by it.

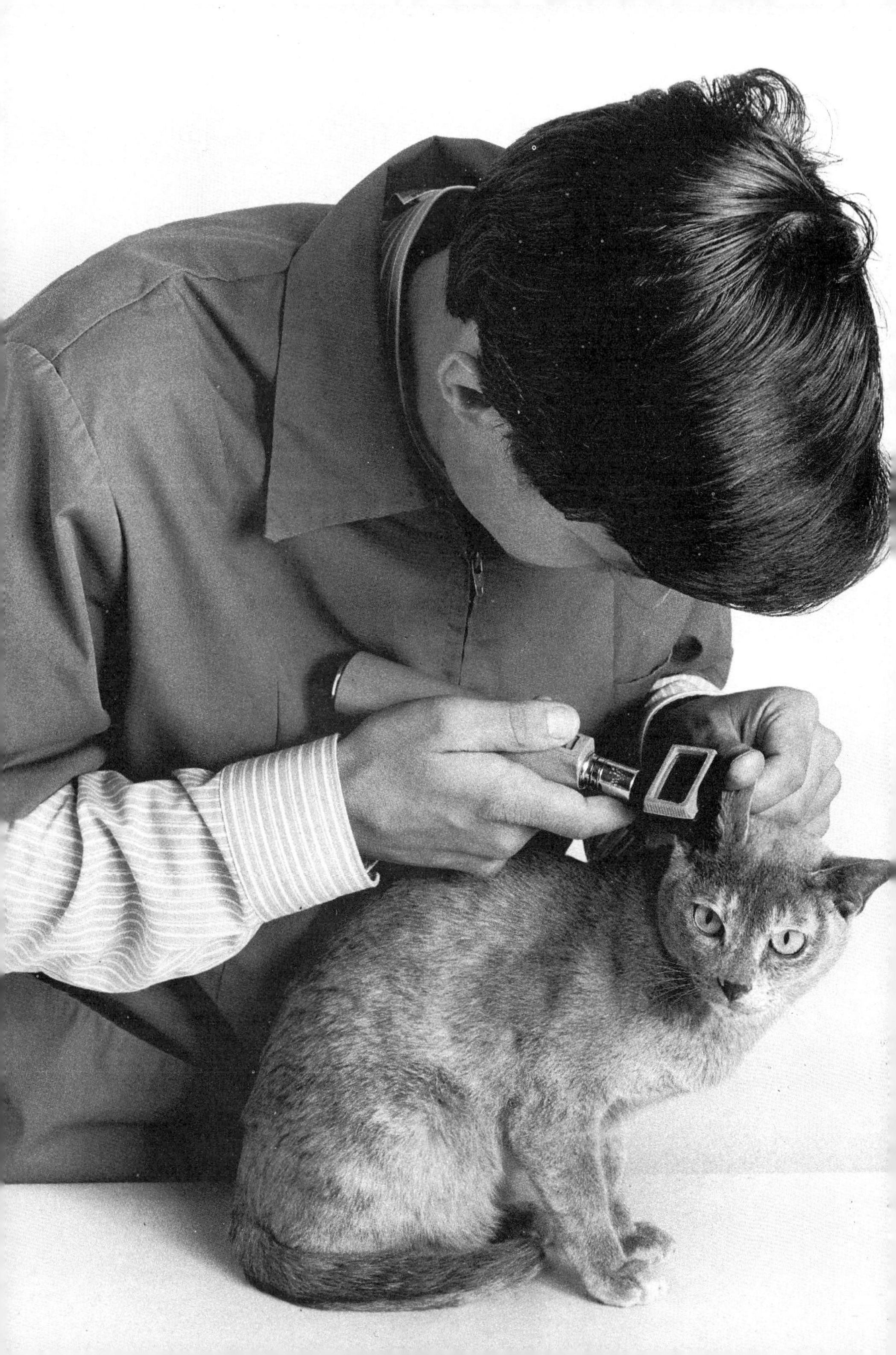

3

HEALTH CARE

The cat's elegant, tough body design goes some way towards confirming the traditional belief that cats have nine lives. However, the cat's natural inquisitiveness, closeness to the ground and ability to explore most nooks and crannies expose it to a broad spectrum of germs. And its size predisposes it to certain types of accident, especially when it is a city dweller. Also, stress or poor condition can lower your cat's resistance to illness, giving disease a chance to attack. You can take precautions to keep your cat healthy, but if it does succumb to illness, you should consult a vet as soon as possible.

How to use this chapter

The chapter begins with information that helps you to decide whether or not your cat is ill, including instructions on taking a cat's temperature and pulse, and diagnosis charts that cover the major signs of ill-health in the cat. This is followed by the ailments and disorders section, which is divided into areas of the body and systems within it. Finally, the care and nursing section provides information on veterinary care, looking after an ill or elderly cat at home, and basic first aid.

Is my cat ill?
Strictly speaking, animals can't display symptoms, as these are sensations and phenomena which can be described *by the patient*. However, a sick or injured cat will show observable phenomena; these are termed "signs".

Is my cat healthy?
A healthy cat's fur is sleek and unbroken, its eyes are clear and bright, and its nostrils are clean and dry (not parched or moist). It has a hearty appetite, and its excretory systems function regularly. It walks fluidly, and moves with purpose and self-possession. It grooms itself regularly with its tongue, purrs at appropriate moments, and shows no sudden flashes of irritation or bizarre behaviour. And handling by humans produces no signs of pain or discomfort.

ZOONOSES

A few cat ailments, known as zoonoses, can affect humans. They are: ☐ Rabies (see p. 15) ☐ skin parasitism (see pp. 83-4) ☐ Toxoplasmosis (see p. 67). However, there are a number of precautions you can take to prevent infection:

- Always wash your hands after touching a pet
- Don't allow pregnant women and young children to touch cat's droppings
- Keep sandpits covered
- Clean all bite and scratch wounds and treat with antiseptic. If pain or swelling develops, seek medical advice as infected wounds can induce "cat scratch fever"
- Keep a cat with ringworm (see p. 84) "in quarantine" in a spare room

AILMENTS SECTION

Quick-reference boxes help you to make decisions when you spot signs of illness.

Urgency advice Crosses indicate how quickly you should contact a vet.

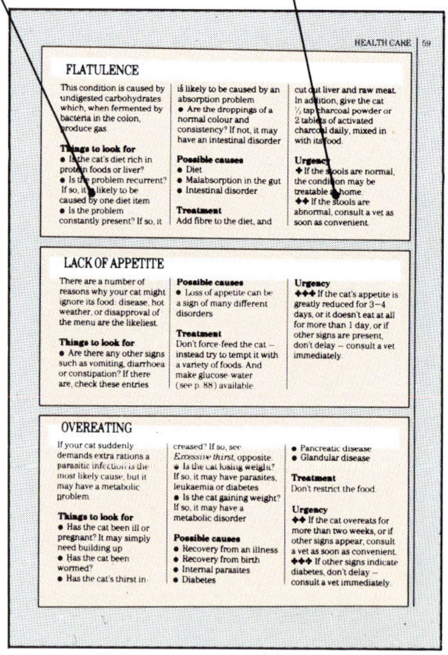
HEALTH CARE | 59

FLATULENCE

This condition is caused by undigested carbohydrates which, when fermented by bacteria in the colon, produce gas.

Things to look for
● Is the cat's diet rich in protein foods or liver?
● Is the problem recurrent? If so, it is likely to be caused by one diet item
● Is the problem constantly present? If so, it is likely to be caused by an absorption problem
● Are the droppings of a normal colour and consistency? If not, it may have an intestinal disorder

Possible causes
● Diet
● Malabsorption in the gut
● Intestinal disorder

Treatment
Add fibre to the diet, and cut out liver and raw meat. In addition, give the cat ½ tsp charcoal powder or 2 tablets of activated charcoal daily, mixed in with its food.

Urgency
✚ If the stools are normal, the condition may be treatable at home.
✚✚ If the stools are abnormal, consult a vet as soon as convenient.

LACK OF APPETITE

There are a number of reasons why your cat might ignore its food: disease, hot weather, or disapproval of the menu are the likeliest.

Things to look for
● Are there any other signs such as vomiting, diarrhoea or constipation? If there are, check these entries

Possible causes
● Loss of appetite can be a sign of many different disorders

Treatment
Don't force-feed the cat – instead try to tempt it with a variety of foods. And make glucose-water (see p. 88) available.

Urgency
✚✚✚ If the cat's appetite is greatly reduced for 3–4 days, or it doesn't eat at all for more than 1 day, or if other signs are present, don't delay – consult a vet immediately.

OVEREATING

If your cat suddenly demands extra rations a parasitic infection is the most likely cause, but it may have a metabolic problem.

Things to look for
● Has the cat been ill or pregnant? It may simply need building up
● Has the cat been wormed?
● Has the cat's thirst increased? If so, see *Excessive thirst*, opposite.
● Is the cat losing weight? If so, it may have parasites, leukaemia or diabetes
● Is the cat gaining weight? If so, it may have a metabolic disorder

Possible causes
● Recovery from an illness
● Recovery from birth
● Internal parasites
● Diabetes
● Pancreatic disease
● Glandular disease

Treatment
Don't restrict the food.

Urgency
✚✚ If the cat overeats for more than two weeks, or if other signs appear, consult a vet as soon as convenient.
✚✚✚ If other signs indicate diabetes, don't delay – consult a vet immediately.

SIGNS OF ILLNESS

The first signs of ill-health you will probably notice in your cat usually involve behaviour: it becomes duller, more introverted and less active. Also, its appetite is often affected – it may decrease or increase.

Warning — acute signs: If your cat displays any of the following signs consult a vet immediately: ☐ collapse ☐ vomiting repeatedly for more than 24 hours ☐ diarrhoea for longer than 24 hours ☐ troubled breathing ☐ bleeding from an orifice ☐ dilated pupils.

Major signs: Looking off colour, Vomiting, Diarrhoea, Abnormal breathing, Bleeding, Scratching (see pp. 39-45).

Other common signs of illness

On close examination, you may be able to detect other signs:

Respiratory signs ☐ Sneezing (see p. 47) ☐ Nasal discharge (see p. 49) ☐ Coughing (see p. 46)

Oral/appetite signs ☐ Drooling (see pp. 50, 60) ☐ Over/undereating (see p. 59) ☐ Increased thirst (see p. 58)

Eye signs ☐ Discharge (see p. 51) ☐ Cloudiness (see p. 52) ☐ Closed lids (see p. 52)

Ear signs ☐ Discharge (see p. 53)

Body signs ☐ Pain when touched (see p. 80) ☐ Limping (see p. 80)

Bowel/urinary signs ☐ Constipation (see p. 58) ☐ Frequent urination (see p. 70) ☐ Straining (see p. 70)

Back-up information
Following the quick-reference boxes, you will find more detailed information on specific problems.

Prevention boxes
Where relevant, preventative measures are given.

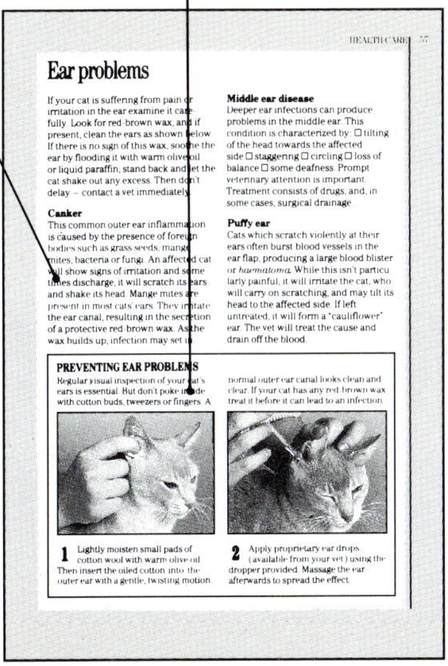

HEALTH CARE | 57

Ear problems

If your cat is suffering from pain or irritation in the ear examine it carefully. Look for red-brown wax, and if present, clean the ears as shown below. If there is no sign of this wax, soothe the ear by flooding it with warm olive oil or liquid paraffin, stand back and let the cat shake out any excess. Then don't delay – contact a vet immediately.

Canker
This common outer ear inflammation is caused by the presence of foreign bodies such as grass seeds, mange mites, bacteria or fungi. An affected cat will show signs of irritation and sometimes discharge, it will scratch its ears and shake its head. Mange mites are present in most cats' ears. They irritate the ear canal, resulting in the secretion of a protective red-brown wax. As the wax builds up, infection may set in.

Middle ear disease
Deeper ear infections can produce problems in the middle ear. This condition is characterized by: ☐ tilting of the head towards the affected side ☐ staggering ☐ circling ☐ loss of balance ☐ some deafness. Prompt veterinary attention is important. Treatment consists of drugs, and, in some cases, surgical drainage.

Puffy ear
Cats which scratch violently at their ears often burst blood vessels in the ear flap, producing a large blood blister or *haematoma*. While this isn't particularly painful, it will irritate the cat, who will carry on scratching, and may tilt its head to the affected side. If left untreated, it will form a "cauliflower" ear. The vet will treat the cause and drain off the blood.

PREVENTING EAR PROBLEMS
Regular visual inspection of your cat's ears is essential. But don't poke inside with cotton buds, tweezers or fingers. A normal outer ear canal looks clean and clear. If your cat has any red-brown wax treat it before it can lead to an infection.

1 Lightly moisten small pads of cotton wool with warm olive oil. Then insert the oiled cotton into the outer ear with a gentle, twisting motion.

2 Apply proprietary ear drops (available from your vet) using the dropper provided. Massage the ear afterwards to spread the effect.

DIAGNOSIS CHARTS

Answer the questions and follow the arrows to an endpoint that suggests a likely veterinary diagnosis.

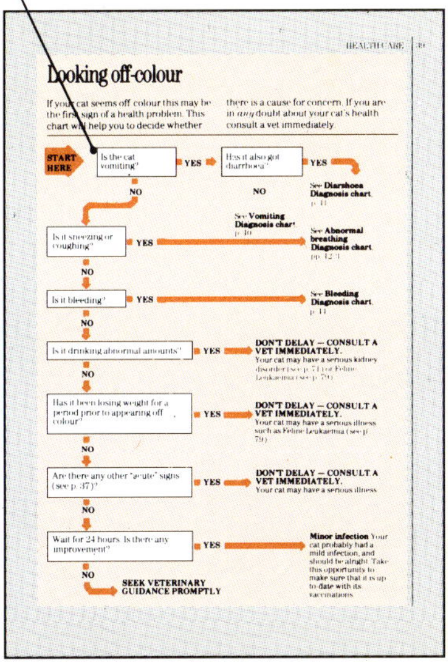

HEALTH CARE | 39

Looking off-colour

If your cat seems off colour this may be the first sign of a health problem. This chart will help you to decide whether there is a cause for concern. If you are in *any* doubt about your cat's health consult a vet immediately.

TAKING A CAT'S TEMPERATURE

If you suspect that your cat is ill, taking its temperature can be useful in assessing its condition. The normal level is about 38.6° C, but this may well fluctuate slightly. However, I don't consider a cat feverish until its temperature is over 39.2° C.

Method
Ask a helper to hold the cat firmly (see below). Using a stubby-ended glass clinical thermometer, shake down the mercury with several sharp flicks of your wrist. Lubricate the glass bulb with liquid paraffin or vegetable oil, lift the cat's tail and insert the thermometer slowly into the anus, until about 2 cms of it is inside the cat. Gently angle the thermometer so that the bulb comes into contact with the wall of the rectum. Hold it in position for about one minute, then withdraw, wipe and read it against the scale.

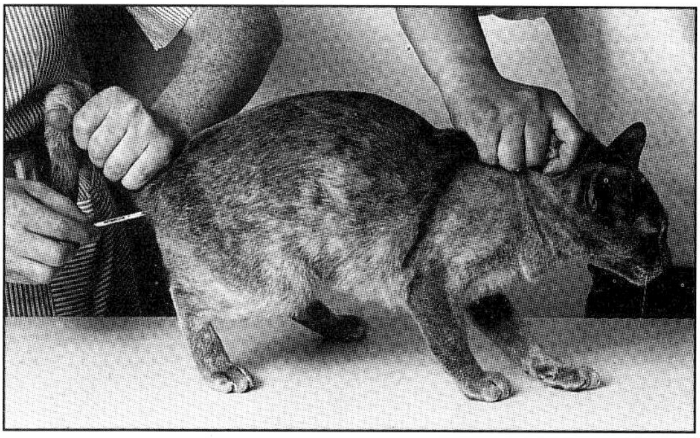

Holding the cat
Get your helper to grasp the cat by its scruff with one hand so that you are free to lift the tail and insert the thermometer.

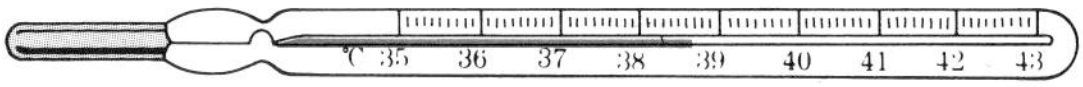

Temperature reading
A healthy cat's temperature is around 38.6° C.

TAKING A CAT'S PULSE

Most cats have a pulse rate of 110–40 beats per minute when at rest. You can detect it by feeling the femoral artery in the groin (see right) and counting the beats. The pulse should be strong and regular.

Finding a pulse
Feel along the inside of the thigh, where the leg meets the body.

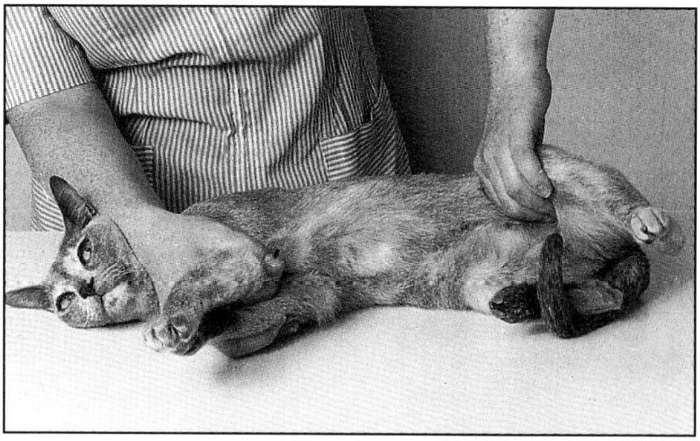

Looking off-colour

If your cat seems off-colour this may be the first sign of a health problem. This chart will help you to decide whether there is a cause for concern. If you are in *any* doubt about your cat's health consult a vet immediately.

START HERE

Is the cat vomiting? **YES** → Has it also got diarrhoea? **YES** → See **Diarrhoea Diagnosis chart**, p. 41.

Has it also got diarrhoea? **NO** → See **Vomiting Diagnosis chart**, p. 40.

Is the cat vomiting? **NO** ↓

Is it sneezing or coughing? **YES** → See **Abnormal breathing Diagnosis chart**, pp. 42-3.

NO ↓

Is it bleeding? **YES** → See **Bleeding Diagnosis chart**, p. 44.

NO ↓

Is it drinking abnormal amounts? **YES** → **DON'T DELAY — CONSULT A VET IMMEDIATELY.** Your cat may have a serious kidney disorder (see p. 71) or Feline Leukaemia (see p. 79).

NO ↓

Has it been losing weight for a period prior to appearing off-colour? **YES** → **DON'T DELAY — CONSULT A VET IMMEDIATELY.** Your cat may have a serious illness such as Feline Leukaemia (see p. 79).

NO ↓

Are there any other "acute" signs (see p. 37)? **YES** → **DON'T DELAY — CONSULT A VET IMMEDIATELY.** Your cat may have a serious illness.

NO ↓

Wait for 24 hours. Is there any improvement? **YES** → **Minor infection** Your cat probably had a mild infection, and should be alright. Take this opportunity to make sure that it is up-to-date with its vaccinations.

NO → **SEEK VETERINARY GUIDANCE PROMPTLY**

Vomiting

There are many causes of vomiting in the cat, ranging from the mild to the very serious. If you are in *any* doubt about your cat's health you should telephone your vet or visit the veterinary surgery immediately.

START HERE

Has the cat been in an accident?

- YES → **DON'T DELAY — CONSULT A VET IMMEDIATELY.** Meanwhile, give appropriate first aid, pp. 90-4.
- NO ↓

Has it also got diarrhoea?

- YES → See **Diarrhoea Diagnosis Chart**, p. 41.
- NO ↓

Does it seem dull and depressed?

- YES → **DON'T DELAY — CONSULT A VET IMMEDIATELY.** The cat may have a serious infection.
- NO ↓

Could it have swallowed hair?

- YES → **Hairballs** Many cats, particularly longhaired types, ingest hair when grooming themselves. This may accumulate in the gut, and the cat will vomit in an attempt to rid itself of the obstruction. For treatment see p. 61.
- NO ↓

Is it likely to have worms?

- YES → **Worms** Various internal parasites can affect cats (see pp. 66-7). Consult your vet as soon as convenient — treatment involves worming drugs.
- NO ↓

Has it eaten in the last 30 minutes and are its pupils dilated?

- YES → **DON'T DELAY — CONSULT A VET IMMEDIATELY.** Your cat may have Key-Gaskell syndrome (see p. 77), a serious disease
- NO ↓

Withhold food overnight, then give a small meal. Has vomiting stopped?

- YES → **Non-serious vomiting** Cats vomit fairly easily, usually for one of the following simple reasons: □ hairballs □ overeating □ ingestion of a wild bird □ dietary upsets □ overexcitement. If your cat is otherwise normal and the problem doesn't recur, there is no cause for concern.
- NO → **SEEK VETERINARY GUIDANCE PROMPTLY**

Diarrhoea

If your cat passes frequent liquid or semi-liquid motions it probably has a minor infection, but there is a possibility of something more serious. If you are in *any* doubt about its health telephone or visit your vet immediately.

START HERE

Are the faeces bloody?
- YES → Does there seem to be more than a few drops of blood?
  - YES → **DON'T DELAY — CONSULT A VET IMMEDIATELY.** Your cat may have a serious illness.
  - NO → Has the cat vomited too?
- NO → Has the cat vomited too?

Has the cat vomited too?
- YES → **DON'T DELAY — CONSULT A VET IMMEDIATELY.** Your cat may be suffering from poisoning (see p. 94) or have a serious illness such as Feline Enteritis (see p. 64).
- NO → Does it seem dull and depressed?

Does it seem dull and depressed?
- YES → **DON'T DELAY — CONSULT A VET IMMEDIATELY.** Your cat may have a serious illness.
- NO → Is it a young kitten that has been given cow's milk?

Is it a young kitten that has been given cow's milk?
- YES → **Milk intolerance** Your kitten probably has an intolerance to milk (see p. 64). Replace milk with water. If the problem persists, consult a vet as soon as convenient.
- NO → Apart from the diarrhoea, is the cat well?

Apart from the diarrhoea, is the cat well?
- YES → **Minor infection** Your cat probably has a mild infection, and should be alright. Take this opportunity to make sure that it is up-to-date with its vaccinations.
- NO → **SEEK VETERINARY GUIDANCE PROMPTLY**

Abnormal breathing

A healthy cat's breathing is quiet and even, and consists of 25–30 breaths per minute. If your cat's breathing doesn't seem normal, it may have a health problem or merely be resting or affected by hot weather or exertion. To ascertain the cause follow this chart. If you are in any doubt about your cat's health you should telephone your vet or visit the veterinary surgery immediately.

START HERE

Is the cat's breathing slow, and fails to improve when the cat is disturbed?

YES → **DON'T DELAY – CONSULT A VET IMMEDIATELY.** Your cat may be suffering from poisoning (see p. 94) or have a serious illness.

NO ↓

Is its breathing slow, but improves when it is disturbed?

YES → **Resting** When resting, cats conserve their energy by slowing down their bodily functions to a basic maintenance level. If your cat seems fit and breathes normally when not resting, there is no cause for concern.

NO ↓

Is the cat breathing heavily after recently exerting itself?

YES → **Normal response to exertion** After exercise, cats breathe rapidly – 60–90 breaths per minute – in order to cool down. If your cat seems otherwise normal, there is no cause for concern.

NO ↓

Is it breathing heavily, and is the weather very hot?

YES → **Normal response to hot weather** Cats have fewer sweat glands than us, and therefore panting is an important way of cooling down when overheated. If your cat seems otherwise normal, there is no cause for concern.

NO ↓

Go to next page

continued from previous page

Is the cat breathing heavily, and is this accompanied by other "acute" signs (see p. 37)?

YES → **DON'T DELAY — CONSULT A VET IMMEDIATELY.** Your cat may have a serious illness.

NO ↓

Is it breathing rapidly, and is it a small kitten that is less than a year old?

YES → **DON'T DELAY — CONSULT A VET IMMEDIATELY.** Your kitten may have a serious illness (a form of leukaemia).

NO ↓

Is it breathing rapidly, and is there evidence of an accident?

YES → **DON'T DELAY — CONSULT A VET IMMEDIATELY.** Meanwhile, give appropriate first aid, pp. 90-4.

NO ↓

Is it breathing rapidly, and has it a nasal and/or eye discharge?

YES → **DON'T DELAY — CONSULT A VET IMMEDIATELY.** Your cat probably has Feline Influenza (see p. 49).

NO ↓

Is it breathing rapidly, but seems otherwise normal?

YES → Does breathing normalize if the cat is left alone?

YES → **Overexcitement** Your cat probably caught a glimpse of a mouse, a dog or an alluring member of the opposite sex! If it seems otherwise normal, there is no cause for concern.

NO ↓ (from either question)

SEEK VETERINARY GUIDANCE PROMPTLY

Bleeding

If your cat is bleeding you must investigate the source and take immediate action as it may need urgent veterinary attention. Advice on applying bandages is given on p. 93.

START HERE

Is the cat bleeding from the mouth?

- **YES** → **DON'T DELAY — CONSULT A VET IMMEDIATELY.** Your cat may have a serious wound in its mouth.
- **NO** ↓

Is it bleeding from the anus?

- **YES** → **DON'T DELAY — CONSULT A VET IMMEDIATELY.** Your cat may have minor damage as a result of a scratch or straining. However, there is a possibility of a serious illness such as Feline Enteritis (see p. 64).
- **NO** ↓

Is it bleeding from the vulva?

- **YES** → **DON'T DELAY — CONSULT A VET IMMEDIATELY.** Your cat may be having a miscarriage or be suffering from a serious gynaecological infection.
- **NO** ↓

Is it bleeding from the penis?

- **YES** → **DON'T DELAY — CONSULT A VET IMMEDIATELY.** Your cat may have minor damage as a result of a fight. However, there is a possibility of a serious bladder infection (see p. 71).
- **NO** ↓

Can you see a wound?

- **YES** → Is the wound longer than 5 mm, infected or near a vital structure?
  - **YES** → **DON'T DELAY — CONSULT A VET IMMEDIATELY.** Your cat will need professional attention.
  - **NO** ↓ (to "Has it any matted hair?")
- **NO** ↓

Has it any matted hair?

- **YES** → **Minor skin wound** Matted hair and the presence of blood is usually a sign of a small wound hidden in the fur. Such a wound may be treatable at home (see p. 93).
- **NO** ↓

SEEK VETERINARY GUIDANCE PROMPTLY

Scratching

If your cat scratches itself persistently it probably has a skin problem or a parasitic infestation. In general, these problems aren't serious, but prompt attention is important for your cat's comfort.

START HERE

Is the cat scratching its ears?
- **YES** → Can you see black, gritty material in the ears?
- **NO** → Can you see insects in the coat?

Can you see black, gritty material in the ears?
- **YES** → **Ear mites** Your cat has an ear mite infestation. You should clean the ears and give appropriate treatment (see p. 57).
- **NO** → Is there a coloured discharge from the ears?

Is there a coloured discharge from the ears?
- **YES** → **DON'T DELAY – CONSULT A VET IMMEDIATELY.** Your cat probably has a bacterial or fungal infection (see p. 57).
- **NO** → Can you see insects in the coat?

Can you see insects in the coat?
- **YES** → Arc the insects grey?
- **NO** → Can you see black, gritty material in the coat?

Arc the insects grey?
- **YES** → **Lice** Your cat is infested with lice. Give appropriate treatment (see p. 83).
- **NO** → Are the insects black?

Are the insects black?
- **YES** → **Fleas** Your cat is infested with fleas. Give appropriate treatment (see p. 83).

Can you see black, gritty material in the coat?
- **YES** → **Fleas**
- **NO** → Is there any hair loss?

Is there any hair loss?
- **YES** → Is the loss on the thighs, back and forelegs?
- **NO** → **SEEK VETERINARY GUIDANCE PROMPTLY**

Is the loss on the thighs, back and forelegs?
- **YES** → **Eczema** Your cat has a skin problem (see p. 82).
- **NO** → Is the cat male, and is the loss around the tail, with crusty skin at its base?

Is the cat male, and is the loss around the tail, with crusty skin at its base?
- **YES** → **Stud tail** This skin problem is fairly common in toms. Consult a vet as soon as convenient.
- **NO** → **SEEK VETERINARY GUIDANCE PROMPTLY**

RESPIRATORY DISORDERS

The most common respiratory problems in cats are due to infection. Although most illnesses turn out to be mild "colds", some cat influenzas can be life- threatening, especially in unvaccinated animals.

COUGHING

A cough is a reflex action brought on by irritation of the air passages.

Things to look for

- Has the cat swallowed something that has stuck in its throat?
- Are there any typical cold or flu signs present: fever, breathing problems, nasal or eye discharges, sneezing?
- Is the cat bringing up phlegm? If so, it may have an acute chest infection
- Does the cough sound "bubbly"? If so, fluid may have built up on the chest from an infection
- Does the cough sound dry and hacking? If so, the cat may have bronchitis
- Are there any pollutants such as cigarette smoke in the atmosphere?

Possible causes

- Obstruction in the throat
- Viral respiratory disease
- Bronchitis
- Allergic reaction
- Reaction to pollutants

Treatment

If the cough was caused by an obstruction administer first aid (see p. 92).

If it was caused by an atmospheric pollutant, air the room.

If the cat has a known allergy, you may be able to give an anti-histamine drug previously prescribed by the vet.

Keep the cat indoors. Cough suppressant medicines aren't advisable.

Urgency

✚ If caused by a transient atmospheric pollutant, it may be treatable at home.

✚✚ If caused by an allergic reaction, consult a vet as soon as convenient.

✚✚✚ In other cases, don't delay – consult a vet immediately.

PANTING

At rest, a cat takes 25–30 breaths a minute. After exercise this rises to 60–90. If you think that your cat is breathing too rapidly, count the rate.

Things to look for

- Is the weather very hot? The cat may simply be trying to cool down
- Are the cat's nostrils obstructed? A blockage may be preventing it from breathing through its nose
- Is there any sign of an accident – the cat may have a chest or lung injury, and/or be in shock
- Has the cat been in a fight? It may have a chest/lung injury, be in shock or frightened
- Are there any signs of respiratory disease such as fever, coughing, nasal or eye discharges or sneezing?

Possible causes

- Hot weather
- Blocked nostrils
- Chest or lung injury
- Shock, fear or stress
- Severe pain
- Viral respiratory disease

Treatment

Keep the cat indoors and handle it as little as possible.

Urgency

✚ If obviously due to overheating, it may be treatable at home.

✚✚✚ In other cases, don't delay – consult a vet immediately.

SHALLOW BREATHING

A cat will breathe shallowly only if breathing more deeply is impossible or causes it pain.

Things to look for

- Has the cat been in an accident? Shallow breathing may be a sign of damage to the chest area
- Has the cat lost its appetite? It may have a severe viral infection
- Are the lips, tongue and gums grey or blue? This is *cyanosis*, and occurs when insufficient oxygen gets into the blood

Possible causes

- Damage to the chest area (the ribs, diaphragm or chest wall) as the result of an accident
- Respiratory infection
- Pleurisy
- Fluid or air in the chest cavity

Treatment

While you wait for the vet, keep the cat indoors in a warm room.

Urgency

✚✚✚ Don't delay – consult a vet immediately.

SNEEZING

Generally associated with respiratory infections, sneezing is a reflex action brought on by irritation in the nasal passages.

Things to look for

- Has the cat a nasal discharge? If so, it probably has an infection of the nostrils or sinuses
- Are any cold or flu signs present: fever, breathing problems, nasal/eye discharges, coughing?

Possible causes

- Bacterial or fungal infection of the nostrils or sinuses
- Viral disease
- Allergic reaction
- Nasal tumour

Treatment

There is little you can do before the vet's examination; keep the cat indoors in a warm, but well-ventilated room. Nasal drops aren't advisable.

Urgency

✚ If no other signs are present, consult a vet when convenient.
✚✚✚ If accompanied by other signs don't delay – consult a vet immediately.

WHEEZING

A whistling sound made on exhalation or inhalation, wheezing is a result of a partial obstruction at some point between the larynx and bronchioles. This narrows the tube, producing the sound much in the same way that the reed of a wind instrument does.

Things to look for

- Are the cat's lips, tongue and gums grey or blue in colour? This occurs when insufficient oxygen gets into the blood. It may indicate a heart problem
- Coughing – this might indicate the presence of lungworms

Possible causes

- Asthma
- Lungworm
- Congestive heart failure
- Tumour in the air passages

Treatment

There is little you can do before the vet's examination; keep the cat indoors in a warm, but well-ventilated room.

Urgency

✚✚✚ Don't delay – consult a vet immediately.

Chest problems

There are several infections that can affect the cat's bronchi and lungs. Only a vet will be able to tell how serious the problem is, so you must arrange for an examination straight away.

Pneumonia

The main signs of pneumonia in a cat are laboured, rapid breathing, often accompanied by loss of appetite and general malaise. If your cat shows these signs don't automatically assume that it has pneumonia as similar signs can be produced by pleurisy. Pneumonia isn't very common in cats, and is generally a complication of severe cat flu. Other causes are: □ bacterial and fungal infections □ inhalation of liquids □ irritation by gases or vapours □ parasites such as lungworms.

What is the treatment?

The diagnosis of pneumonia may include taking X-rays, swabs and/or blood samples, and withdrawing a sample of fluid from the chest. Treatment will depend on the diagnosis.

Pleurisy

Fairly common in cats, pleurisy is a build-up of milky, often purulent fluid in the chest cavity that compresses the lung and makes breathing difficult. The cause is sometimes a blood-borne bacterial infection, but in a large number of cases the causative factor isn't known.

What is the treatment?

For diagnosis and treatment see Pneumonia.

Other chest conditions

Other conditions may produce similar signs to those of pneumonia and pleurisy. They are: □ rupture of the diaphragm □ penetrating wounds of the chest wall □ haemorrhage into the chest □ bruising of the lungs.

Bronchitis

This condition is usually indicated by a cough, and is caused by inflammation of the air tubes (bronchi) that link the windpipe to the lungs. Causes include: □ irritants such as gases or smoke □ foreign bodies □ infections.

What is the treatment?

Treatment of bronchitis depends on the cause, but in all cases will probably include drugs to dilate the bronchi and dissolve thick secretions.

Lungworms

These tiny parasites are often found in cats' lungs, particularly in country areas. Most cats don't show any signs of infestation, though a few may have a chronic, dry cough. In general, affected cats get rid of the lungworm parasite of their own accord, but in a severe case drug treatment may be necessary.

Asthma

Asthmatic attacks are characterized by heavy, distressed breathing, wheezing, and in severe cases the development of a blue tinge to the tongue, gums, and lips (often combined with the animal's collapse). As in humans, the cause of this condition isn't fully understood, but an allergic sensitivity is a major factor.

What is the treatment?

Attacks can be relieved by drugs which open up the bronchial tubes to ease breathing.

Upper respiratory problems

Cats often seem to have identical respiratory problems to humans: coughing, sneezing, watery eyes, runny nose, looking "rotten", and breathing changes. Often, these problems are signs of a mild illness, and will clear up in a few days with careful nursing. However, they can be signs of a more severe, even fatal infection, that requires prompt veterinary treatment. Only a vet will be able to tell how serious the infection is, so in such cases you must arrange for an immediate examination.

Viral diseases

Cats don't suffer from human viruses; they have their own range of respiratory germs, some mild and some dangerous. Just as human "flu" can appear in a strain that causes more fatalities than usual, so too can feline viruses. At least three viruses and one other germ *(rickettsia)* can produce inflammation of the cat's upper respiratory system – a condition known as Feline Influenza or "Cat Flu". Of these viruses, the two most important are *feline viral rhinotracheitis* (FVRV) and *feline calici* (FCV).

Feline viral rhinotracheitis virus

FVRV is the more serious of the two major viruses. After a 2–10 day incubation period it produces inflammation of the eye, nose and windpipe, with resultant discharges. The cat becomes apathetic and feverish,

PREVENTING CAT FLU

The main way of preventing feline influenza lies in the use of vaccines. These are very reliable, though they don't give 100 percent protection – very virulent strains of flu can sometimes break through their defences to produce mild signs of disease, and a very occasional cat doesn't react in the normal way when injected with the vaccine, failing to become immune.

As well as having your cat vaccinated, you should try to avoid taking it to places where the risk of infection is high. In my view, catteries are the biggest danger spots. If you can't get a helpful neighbour to visit your cat at home while you are away, and you have to use a cattery, choose carefully. First and foremost, you must make sure that you pick one that insists on guests having been vaccinated before they arrive, and demands certificates as proof.

Getting your cat vaccinated

Ask your vet at what age your kitten should be vaccinated. Normally, kittens don't receive their first flu shot until they are about nine weeks old. This is followed by a second shot 3–4 weeks later. Kittens under nine weeks old will still retain maternal flu antibody in their blood, and this would interfere with the development of immunity. However, when there is a high risk of infection your vet may recommend that a younger kitten is vaccinated.

Vaccine checklist

To keep your cat healthy, remember the following:

- All cats need an annual booster dose.
- If your cat is pregnant, she must be given dead or inactivated vaccine, *never* the live sort.
- Only healthy cats should be vaccinated.
- No animal is protected by vaccine until one week after its second dose.

loses its appetite, and sneezes continually. As the secondary bacteria move in, the discharges from the eyes and nostrils become thicker and purulent, and sometimes the cat develops painful ulcers on its tongue. Pneumonia, pleurisy and miscarriage of pregnant queens may also follow. The mortality rate for affected kittens and elderly cats is high.

Feline calici virus
The FCV germ produces signs that can range from a state that is almost as severe as that of an FVRV-infected cat, to a very mild infection indeed, with just a runny nose and moderate sneezing for a few days. It produces tongue ulcers which cause excess salivation, interfere with eating and cause a marked loss of weight and condition. FCV tends not to affect the eyes or nose very dramatically, though some strains are associated with pneumonia.

Reovirus
This third virus is much less serious than the first two. It causes a very mild "cold", and is very rarely fatal.

How cat flu is transmitted
Respiratory viruses come from other cats, and unlike some viruses (such as foot and mouth disease), they can't live long outside the body. FVRV can live for a day away from feline cells, and FCV for about three days. The main way that a virus is transmitted is by contact with an infected cat. Cat shows, catteries, and vets' surgeries are particularly risky places. Apart from the chance of a "carrier" being there, because of the large numbers of cats present, there is also the possibility that a high concentration of virus particles exists, shed by cats passing through. And because a strange environment is more than likely to cause stress, your cat's resistance to viruses will be lowered.

Cats which have recovered completely from cat flu can become carriers, and pass on the virus virtually indefinitely. Others may be left with chronic catarrh of the nasal cavities. In the main, these "snuffles" cases suffer from a recurrent secondary bacterial infection, but they too may be able to pass on the virus.

What is the professional treatment?
The vet will prescribe antibiotics for secondary bacterial infections, and anti-inflammatory drugs for any inflammation. In addition, the cat may be given vitamin and/or hormone injections to boost its recuperative abilities.

What is the home treatment?
Once the cat has been seen by the vet and appropriate treatment given, its successful recovery relies on careful home nursing (see pp. 88–9).

Clearing the nose and eyes
Cats find breathing through their mouths unnatural and troublesome, and since they can't blow into a handkerchief, they rely on you to keep their nostrils clear. Wipe around the nose several times a day, using a damp cotton pad. If necessary, ask the vet to prescribe a nasal decongestant. After cleansing, grease the nose tip with petroleum jelly. And don't allow the cat's eyes to "gum up"; clean them with warm water on damp cotton wool. If the cat's eyes are very inflamed, ask the vet for eye drops.

EYE AND EAR DISORDERS

Of the number of eye and ear problems found in cats, the most serious are blindness and deafness. However, the chances of a sighted or hearing cat going blind or deaf are small, and the most common problem you are likely to encounter is obstruction – foreign matter in the eye or wax in the ear. When treating a cat's eyes or ears, you may find that you need to restrain it (see p. 86). Once it is held still, use a torch and a magnifying glass for the examination.

EYE AND EAR PROBLEMS IN ELDERLY CATS

An elderly cat's hearing and eyesight may fail gradually. If this happens to your pet, remember that a deaf cat can't hear potential dangers such as a vacuum cleaner. With a blind cat, keep its feeding bowls in the same place, avoid rearranging familiar furniture, and protect it from dangers such as open fires.

BULGING EYE

Swelling of the tissue behind the eye will push the cat's eyeball forward, making it protrude out of the socket.

Things to look for
- Protruding eyeball
- Staring look
- Eyelid won't close
- Dilated pupil – due to stretched nerves to eye

Possible causes
- Accidental blow
- Infection spread from sinus
- Tumour behind eyeball
- Glaucoma

Treatment
There is very little you can do before the vet's examination; just keep the cat indoors.

Urgency
+++ Don't delay – consult a vet immediately. To reduce the swelling, drugs, or perhaps surgery, will be needed.

DISCHARGE FROM THE EYES

A clear discharge is often caused by blocked tear ducts, and is fairly common, particularly in Longhairs. Less common but more serious is a cloudy discharge, probably due to an infection.

Things to look for
- Is the discharge clear? If so, the cat probably has blocked tear ducts
- Is the discharge cloudy? If so, the cat may well have a bacterial or viral infection
- Are the cat's eyes also causing it pain? If so, see *Painful eye* (p. 52)

Possible causes
- Blocked tear ducts
- Conjunctivitis
- Viral respiratory illness
- Eye disease such as glaucoma

Treatment
Don't let the discharge mat into the cat's fur – bathe the area around its eye with warm water on cotton.

Urgency
++ If clear, seek veterinary advice as soon as convenient.
+++ If purulent or painful, don't delay – consult a vet immediately.

FAILING SIGHT

This condition can't be detected from looking at the eye; you are more likely to suspect it from observing the cat's behaviour. If you think that your cat might have vision problems, try the test on the right, testing one eye at a time.

Things to look for

- Is the cat's coordination impaired?
- Is the cat bumping into furniture?
- Does the cat's eye(s) look cloudy? If so, it may have a serious infection of the eye
- Does the cat respond to a moving object?

Testing sight
Cover one eye and move your finger towards the other, as if you were going to touch it. If the cat blinks, it has some sight in that eye.

Possible causes

- Diseases such as retinal disease, cataract, keratitis or glaucoma
- Processes affecting the brain such as encephalitis caused by an infection, a stroke, a tumour, or an inherited neurological disease

Treatment

Prompt veterinary attention is important. Meanwhile, keep the cat indoors in familar surroundings, and put a guard in front of fires.

Urgency

✚✚✚ Don't delay – consult a vet immediately. Total or partial loss of sight may be reversible with prompt treatment.

PAINFUL EYE

A foreign body in the eye, accidental injury or disease can affect a cat's eyes. The main sign of these problems is usually pain or discomfort.

Things to look for

- Does the cat keep its eyelid closed? It may have an irritant infection or a corneal abrasion
- Is the cat pawing at its eye? It may have an irritant infection or a foreign body in its eye
- Is there a blue or white opacity in or on the eye? This may indicate that the cat has a cataract
- Is there any discharge? If so, see *Discharge from the eyes* (p. 51)

Possible causes

- Foreign body in the eye
- Conjunctivitis
- Severe infection such as glaucoma
- Cataract
- Accidental abrasion
- Tumour
- Congenital disease

Treatment

In all cases, you can help the cat by gently flooding or bathing its eyes with a soothing liquid solution. The best way to do this is to soak a pad of cotton in cold tea or a solution of 1 tsp of boracic acid in 1 cup of warm water, and squeeze the liquid into the cat's eye.

If the eye is bleeding, you should hold a pad of cotton wool soaked in iced water onto it until the vet can examine it.

Bathing a cat's eye
Use a cotton pad to gently squeeze a suitably soothing liquid onto the eye.

Urgency

✚✚✚ Don't delay – consult a vet immediately.

DEAFNESS

A hearing cat turns its head to look in the direction of a sound, moving its ears around to locate the exact position of a noise. If your cat doesn't do this, it may well be deaf. This condition may be either temporary or permanent, depending on the cause. Hereditary or degenerative factors and inner ear disease generally produce permanent deafness, whilst deafness brought on by outer and middle ear infections, wax or parasites may be temporary. Cats generally cope well with deafness.

Things to look for

- Are there signs of a build-up of wax in the ear? If so, the ear canal may be blocked
- Is there any sign of irritation, soreness or discharge (see below)? This would indicate an outer or middle ear infection
- Is the cat holding its head to one side? This would indicate a middle or inner ear infection
- Is the cat white in colour? It may have hereditary deafness
- Is it old? It may have a degenerative problem

Possible causes

- Wax blockage
- Outer ear infection
- Middle ear infection
- Inner ear infection
- Hereditary factor
- Old age

Treatment

There is little you can do before the vet's examination.

Urgency

✚✚ Seek veterinary advice as soon as convenient. The vet will check the ears for the presence of wax, infection, tumours or parasites.

DISCHARGE FROM THE EARS

This common problem is generally a sign of a bacterial infection or a parasitic infestation. Often, such problems can be prevented by regularly inspecting and cleaning your cat's outer ear area (see p. 57).

Things to look for

- Is the discharge dark and waxy? If so, the cat may have an ear mite or fungal infestation
- Is the discharge purulent? If so, the cat may have a bacterial infection
- Is the cat shaking its head? This would indicate an ear mite infestation

Possible causes

- Ear mites
- Bacterial infection
- Fungal infection

Treatment

Gently clean the outer ear area, using a twist of cotton wool soaked in warm olive oil (see below). Don't let the discharge mat into the cat's fur – bathe the surrounding area with warm water, then dry it carefully.

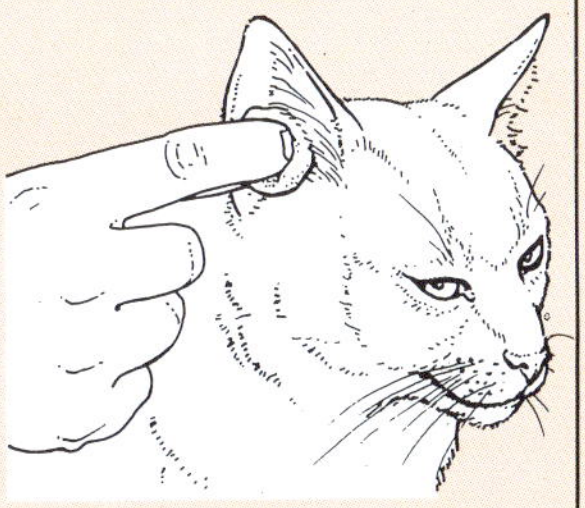

Cleaning the ear
Wipe the outer ear area clean with a gentle, circular motion.

Discourage the cat from scratching its ear – it may develop a large blood blister known as a haemotoma (see p. 57).

Don't probe down into the ear canal with any object, not even your fingers.

Urgency

✚✚ Seek veterinary advice as soon as convenient.

Eye problems

There are several signs which indicate an eye disorder: □ partial or total closure of the eye □ swelling and inflammation of the eyelid □ covering of part or all of the eye by the third eyelid □ profuse watering or discharge □ cloudiness or blueness of the normally transparent cornea □ changes of colour deeper in the eye □ swelling of the eyeball □ blood in the eye itself □ blood oozing from the eyelid □ signs of blindness (see p. 52). If you observe any of these signs, singly or in combination, apply first aid and don't delay in contacting a vet as expert treatment is essential for *all* eye problems.

Scratched eyelid or eye

The most common cause of damage to the eyelids or eye itself is a scratch from another cat. At first, the cat will display: □ soreness □ watering □ blinking □ closure of the eyelids. This may lead to an infection, resulting in: □ swollen eyelids □ purulent discharge. And, if the eyeball is affected: □ ulceration or inflammation of the cornea.

Conjunctivitis

Inflammation of the lining of the eyelids and the thin layer of tissue covering the visible white of the eyeball is known as conjunctivitis. Signs include: □ redness □ watering or discharge □ soreness □ blinking □ closure of the lids. Conjunctivitis can be caused by: □ bacterial infection □ upper respiratory viruses (see p. 49) □ congenitally inturned eyelids □ allergic reaction □ a foreign body □ irritant gases, vapours, smoke or liquids □ an eye worm known as *Thelazia*.

Conjunctivitis
There are several possible causes for the inflammation and discharge affecting this cat's eye. In all such cases prompt veterinary attention is essential.

Corneal problems

The normally transparent "window" of the eye may be damaged by a blow or infected by bacteria, becoming cloudy and bluish, and later white and opaque. This is *not* the same thing as a cataract. Simple, non-infected corneal wounds heal quickly, but where infection is present, ulceration or further inflammation deeper in the eye may follow.

Ulcers on the cornea can be caused by wounds, particularly in breeds like Longhairs which have prominent eyes. Alternatively, they can be caused by an infection, such as the FVRV virus (see p. 49).

A black area of dead cells in the centre of the cornea, the cause of which is unknown, occasionally occurs in Longhairs, producing watering and associated conjunctivitis.

Conditions of the inner eye

Inflammation of the iris itself, the choroid and its associated muscles can be due to a number of causes, including: □ penetrating wounds □ corneal ulcerations □ infections such as Feline Infectious Peritonitis or Toxoplasmosis.

Retinal inflammation also has many causes, from tuberculosis to Toxoplasmosis. And a blow can detach part of the retina, leading to partial blindness.

Glaucoma

This serious condition involves enlargement of the eye, often with attendant corneal cloudiness, and occurs when the fluid within the eye can't circulate as a result of internal bleeding, inflammation of the iris and associated structures, or a tumour.

Cataracts

Opacity of the pupil of a cat's eye is often due to the development of a cataract in the lens, and generally occurs in elderly or diabetic cats. Apparent opacity of the lens in elderly cats isn't necessarily a cataract – it may be merely a change in the refractive index of the lens due to age. This doesn't interfere with normal vision.

Third eyelid problems

The "haw", nictating membrane or "third eyelid" is a little triangle of pink or white tissue that peeps out from the inner corner of each eye. Sometimes one of these "eyelids" is damaged in a fight. Once swollen and inflamed, it protrudes at the corner of the eye, and in such cases it is best dealt with by the vet under anaesthetic.

Often a worried owner will take a cat to the vet because it has suddenly developed "white sheets" over its eyes. What has happened is that the third eyelid has moved over a portion of the cornea. The cat is *not* blind as a result, but it certainly makes the cat look very odd. The cause of this common complaint isn't fully understood. It is likely that a debilitating factor such as a virus either makes the eyeball muscles contract into the socket or the pad of fat behind the eye shrink in size so that the eyeball settles back, pushing the third eyelid forward. Often a generalized condition lies behind it: incipient cat flu, diarrhoea or a parasitic infestation.

Eyeball abnormalities

A tumour or a foreign body in the eye can cause a non-congenital squint in any breed of cat, whilst a congenital squint is generally seen in Siamese. Another eye problem peculiar to Siamese produces a rhythmic oscillation of the eyeball. This may be congenital, or the result of an ear

Glaucoma
An opaque, cloudy look to the eye, often accompanied by protrusion, is the most common sign of this disorder.

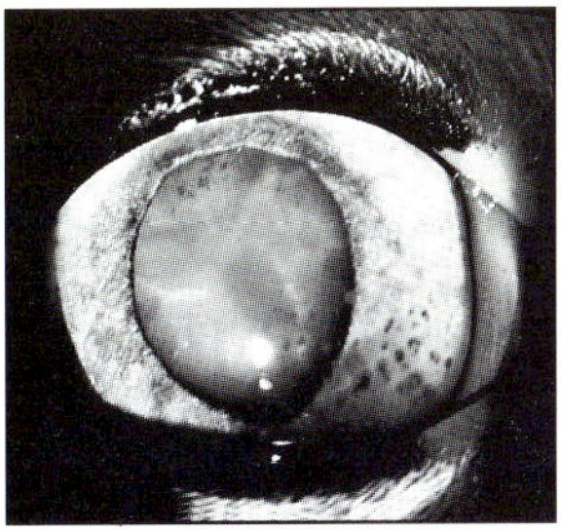

Cataract
Opacity restricted to the pupil is usually a sign of a cataract on the lens. Surgery is only recommended if cataracts affect both eyes.

Protruding third eyelids
This cat's third eyelids or nictating membranes are clearly visible protruding across the eyeballs from the inner corners of its eyes.

APPLYING OINTMENT TO A CAT'S EYELID

Hold your cat's head still with one hand and use the other to apply the ointment. Only use a proprietary ointment for cats that has been prescribed by your vet.

And don't apply any form of eye ointment to your cat's eyes before visiting the vet as it may interfere with the examination.

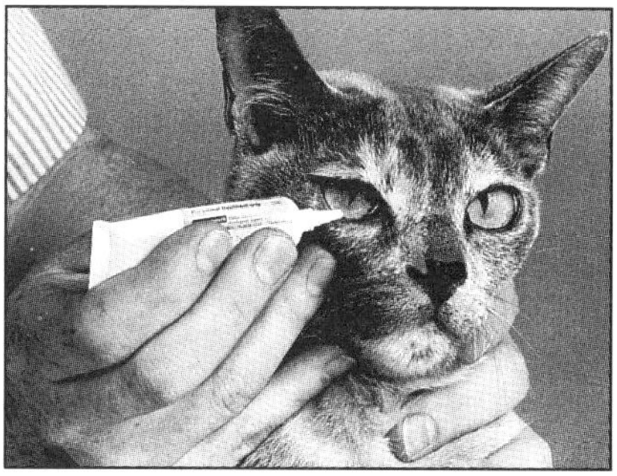

1 Hold the tube parallel with the eye, *not* pointing towards it. Squeeze it, allowing a line of ointment to fall across and into contact with the eyeball.

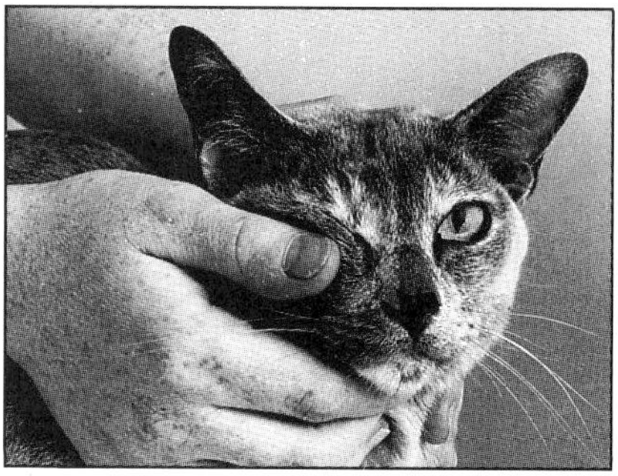

2 Hold the eyelids gently together for a few moments to allow the ointment to melt onto the eye.

disorder such as middle ear disease or a brain condition like a stroke.

Blindness

Severe eye conditions such as infected ulcers on both corneas will drastically affect vision. However, evidence of blindness (see p. 52) is sometimes seen in a cat which displays no obvious signs of eye disease or damage. Such cases are caused by changes in the deep structure of the eye, in the visual centre of the brain or the nerves linking eye to brain. Expert examination is urgently needed as some cases respond to speedy treatment.

Gradually developing blindness in a cat which knows its own home can be coped with. The cat has time to adjust to its loss of sight, and still enjoy life. Though obviously, it can't be allowed outdoors. However, a cat that turns blind suddenly can become very disturbed. In such a case, if the vet advises that the condition is irreversible, euthanasia is the most humane course.

What is the treatment for eye problems?

When you notice any signs of eye trouble in your cat *don't* delay – contact a vet immediately. Meanwhile, you can help your pet by removing matted discharges and bathing "gummed-up" eyelids. Swab the affected area gently and repeatedly with warm human eye wash or tea. Don't apply any form of eye ointment before visiting the vet as it may interfere with the examination. And don't use eyedrops prescribed for humans without your vet's permission. Some problems such as infections require drug therapy; others, like cataracts, require an operation.

Ear problems

If your cat is suffering from pain or irritation in the ear examine it carefully. Look for red-brown wax, and if present, clean the ears as shown below. If there is no sign of this wax, soothe the ear by flooding it with warm olive oil or liquid paraffin, stand back and let the cat shake out any excess. Then don't delay – contact a vet immediately.

Canker

This common outer ear inflammation is caused by the presence of foreign bodies such as grass seeds, mange mites, bacteria or fungi. An affected cat will show signs of irritation and sometimes discharge, it will scratch its ears and shake its head. Mange mites are present in most cats' ears. They irritate the ear canal, resulting in the secretion of a protective red-brown wax. As the wax builds up, infection may set in.

Middle ear disease

Deeper ear infections can produce problems in the middle ear. This condition is characterized by: □ tilting of the head towards the affected side □ staggering □ circling □ loss of balance □ some deafness. Prompt veterinary attention is important. Treatment consists of drugs, and, in some cases, surgical drainage.

Puffy ear

Cats which scratch violently at their ears often burst blood vessels in the ear flap, producing a large blood blister or *haematoma*. While this isn't particularly painful, it will irritate the cat, who will carry on scratching, and may tilt its head to the affected side. If left untreated, it will form a "cauliflower" ear. The vet will treat the cause and drain off the blood.

PREVENTING EAR PROBLEMS

Regular visual inspection of your cat's ears is essential. But don't poke inside with cotton buds, tweezers or fingers. A normal outer ear canal looks clean and clear. If your cat has any red-brown wax treat it before it can lead to an infection.

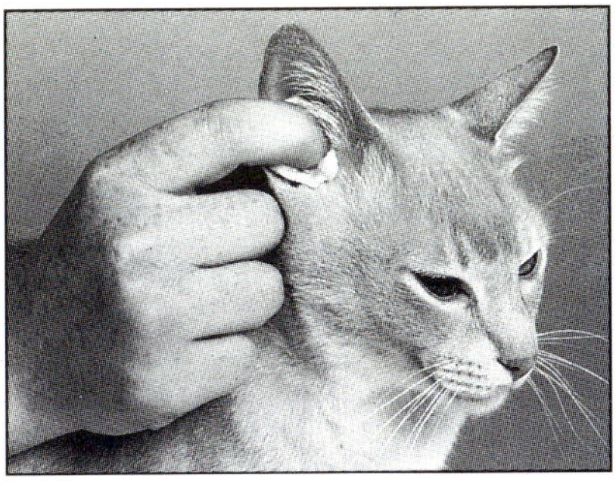

1 Lightly moisten small pads of cotton wool with warm olive oil. Then insert the oiled cotton into the outer ear with a gentle, twisting motion.

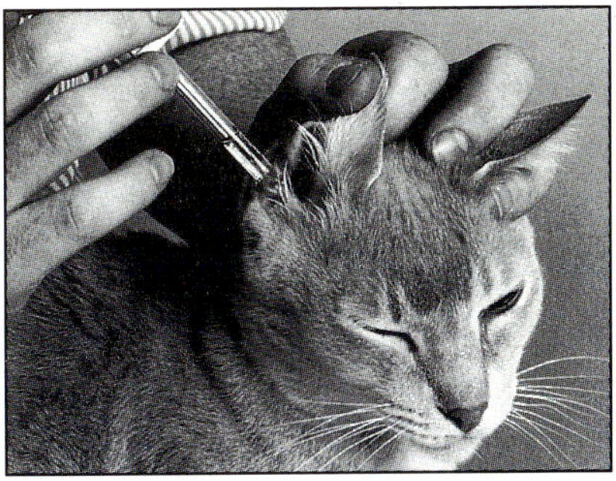

2 Apply proprietary ear drops (available from your vet) using the dropper provided. Massage the ear afterwards to spread the effect.

DIGESTIVE DISORDERS

A cat's digestive system comprises the passageway from mouth to anus, as well as the liver, pancreas, stomach and intestines. The most common problems affecting this system are vomiting, diarrhoea, constipation, loss of appetite, loss of weight and swelling of the abdomen. These have a number of potential causes, some unimportant, some life-threatening, so examination by a vet is essential. Nutritional problems are unusual, and when they do occur they are generally allergic reactions to food. The most common allergy in cats is to cow's milk.

CONSTIPATION

A healthy cat usually opens its bowels once or twice a day. Difficulty in passing stools occurs for one of two reasons: the passage is obstructed or the stool is too hard.

Things to look for

- Are stools hard and dark? This indicates insufficient fluid present
- Is the cat straining, but not passing stools? If normal stools are present, it may have a urinary tract problem (see p. 70)
- Is the cat lethargic? This indicates lack of condition due to poor diet
- Is the cat longhaired? Its intestines may be blocked by a hairball
- Is the cat vomiting? It may have a serious intestinal blockage

Possible causes

- Low water intake
- Incorrect diet
- Lack of exercise
- Old age (weaker abdominal muscles)
- Hairballs
- Intestinal blockage

Treatment

Add dry cat food or bran to the diet to increase the fibre content.

Urgency

✚ If the problem is due to diet, it may be treatable at home.

✚✚ If a diet change has little effect, consult a vet as soon as convenient.

✚✚✚ If the cat is vomiting, don't delay – consult a vet immediately.

EXCESSIVE THIRST

If you notice your cat drinking markedly more water than usual it may have a serious health problem.

Things to look for

- Has the cat's appetite increased too? It may be diabetic
- Has the cat lost weight? This is a serious sign
- Is the cat being treated with cortisone drugs?
- Is the cat vomiting too? This is a serious sign
- In a queen, has she had kittens? If not, she may have a uterine abscess

Possible causes

- Diabetes
- Corticosteroid therapy
- Kidney or liver disease
- Hormone disease
- Certain toxic conditions
- Uterine abscess

Treatment

Don't restrict liquids.

Urgency

✚✚✚ Don't delay – consult a vet immediately.

FLATULENCE

This condition is caused by undigested carbohydrates which, when fermented by bacteria in the colon, produce gas.

Things to look for

- Is the cat's diet rich in protein foods or liver?
- Is the problem recurrent? If so, it is likely to be caused by one diet item
- Is the problem constantly present? If so, it is likely to be caused by an absorption problem
- Are the droppings of a normal colour and consistency? If not, it may have an intestinal disorder

Possible causes

- Diet
- Malabsorption in the gut
- Intestinal disorder

Treatment

Add fibre to the diet, and cut out liver and raw meat. In addition, give the cat ½ tsp charcoal powder or 2 tablets of activated charcoal daily, mixed in with its food.

Urgency

✚ If the stools are normal, the condition may be treatable at home.
✚✚ If the stools are abnormal, consult a vet as soon as convenient.

LACK OF APPETITE

There are a number of reasons why your cat might ignore its food: disease, hot weather, or disapproval of the menu are the likeliest.

Things to look for

- Are there any other signs such as vomiting, diarrhoea or constipation? If there are, check these entries

Possible causes

- Loss of appetite can be a sign of many different disorders

Treatment

Don't force-feed the cat – instead try to tempt it with a variety of foods. And make glucose-water (see p. 88) available.

Urgency

✚✚✚ If the cat's appetite is greatly reduced for 3–4 days, or it doesn't eat at all for more than 1 day, or if other signs are present, don't delay – consult a vet immediately.

OVEREATING

If your cat suddenly demands extra rations a parasitic infection is the most likely cause, but it may have a metabolic problem.

Things to look for

- Has the cat been ill or pregnant? It may simply need building up
- Has the cat been wormed?
- Has the cat's thirst increased? If so, see *Excessive thirst*, opposite.
- Is the cat losing weight? If so, it may have parasites, leukaemia or diabetes
- Is the cat gaining weight? If so, it may have a metabolic disorder

Possible causes

- Recovery from an illness
- Recovery from birth
- Internal parasites
- Diabetes
- Pancreatic disease
- Glandular disease

Treatment

Don't restrict the food.

Urgency

✚✚ If the cat overeats for more than two weeks, or if other signs appear, consult a vet as soon as convenient.
✚✚✚ If other signs indicate diabetes, don't delay – consult a vet immediately.

Problems in the mouth

Health troubles in your cat's mouth will probably come to your notice when one or more of the following signs are exhibited: □ bad breath □ pawing at the mouth □ chattering the teeth when attempting to bite □ excessive salivation □ difficulty in eating.

Pain or discomfort in the teeth, gums or tongue are responsible, and can be caused by a number of abnormalities.

PREVENTING TOOTH DECAY

To prevent a build-up of tartar a cat's teeth must be kept clean. Many cats will agree to having their teeth cleaned once a week with a soft toothbrush, salt and water. If the cat resists, take it to the vet about once a year to have its teeth "descaled" under sedative or an anaesthetic.

Cleaning your cat's teeth

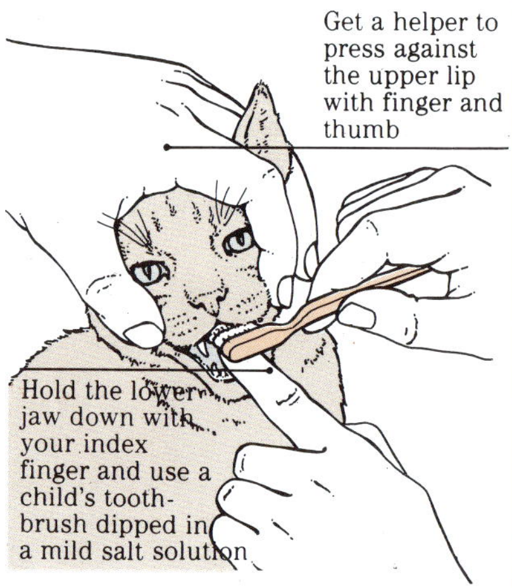

Tooth decay

The modern cat's diet of minced, tinned food may have a detrimental effect on its teeth. Wild cats clean and polish their teeth as they cut through the skin and gristle of fresh carcasses, but giving your cat bones won't have the same effect. Although the sort of decay (caries) we suffer from is very rare in felines, they do have a tendency to accumulate tartar or scale around their teeth. Soft at first and hardening later, this deposit has a high calcium content and is mainly due to the milk and cereal elements of a cat's diet. The main effect of an accumulation of tartar is on the gums, encouraging inflammation (gingevitis), and enabling germs to enter the socket. Slowly, the infection creeps down the socket creating peridontal disease. As a result, the tooth may become loose, the nerve will die and extraction will be necessary.

Gingevitis

There are several causes of gum inflammation: □ tartar □ licking of irritant chemicals □ kidney disease □ vitamin B deficiency □ Leukaemia. At first, the only sign may be a dark red line bordering the teeth. Later, more extensive areas of gum become sore, tender, and a dirty red colour. Ulceration may also occur.

Swelling of the tongue or lip

A translucent swelling beneath one or both sides of the tongue is known as a *ranula*, and is usually noticed when a cat exhibits temporary difficulty in eating. It is caused by a blockage of saliva ducts. And a chronic, gradually expanding slow-to-heal ulcer or swelling on a cat's lip is usually an *eosinophilic granuloma* (a "rodent ulcer"), the cause of which isn't understood. Both these problems can be successfully treated by your vet.

Gullet and stomach problems

The most common health problems affecting the gullet and stomach are obstruction by foreign bodies (see p. 92), and balls of swallowed hair in the stomach.

Problems of the gullet

Inflammation of the gullet is induced by the passage of a foreign body, an irritant poison, or, more rarely, a tumour. Signs are pain and difficulty in swallowing. An affected cat will need immediate veterinary attention as it will gradually become seriously dehydrated.

What is the treatment?

One of the first aims of treatment will be to replace the body's lost fluids, probably by injection. The vet will take steps to neutralize and/or eliminate any poisons or remove any foreign body (see pp. 92-4), and repair any damage to the gullet. Oesophagal tumours are very serious, and euthanasia (see p. 87) is usually advisable.

Gastritis

Vomiting, thirst, a miserable expression, and little else in the way of signs is often diagnosed as gastritis. Pure gastritis – inflammation limited to the wall of the stomach – is rare, and usually caused by the ingestion of poisons or irritant chemicals. A milder form, where the cat seems healthy except for a tendency to regurgitate food after eating, is often referred to as "indigestion". This problem may well be caused by hairballs. In the Southern U.S., the presence of *Spirocerca* worms in the stomach wall may be a factor.

What is the treatment for severe cases?

If the vomiting, thirst and malaise are severe, immediate veterinary help is essential. While you wait for the vet, withdraw solid food and milk. If the cat is thirsty, provide small, frequent "doses" of sweetened, warm water. Also, spoon in ½ tsp of a human anti-acid.

What is the treatment for mild cases?

If your cat has mild indigestion, give it frequent small meals made from fresh, high-quality ingredients. Dose it with one tsp of liquid paraffin daily for three days, and groom it at least once a day. Human anti-acid tablets may be effective – give the cat ½–1 tablet three times a day.

Hairball blockage

Cats who groom themselves very frequently are prone to swallow hairs which gradually build up into a soggy, dark-coloured mass in the stomach. If the furball isn't regurgitated or passed through the intestine certain signs may develop. First, the cat becomes constantly hungry, but is easily filled – no sooner has it taken a mouthful than it walks off apparently replete, but it soon returns again, looking peckish. Eventually, poor condition and weight loss are apparent.

What is the treatment?

Although surgical intervention is necessary in a few cases, the vast majority of cats can be treated at home. Dosing with liquid paraffin will result in the mass either being regurgitated or passed in the faeces. Give three tsp the first day, two tsp the second day and one the third day. Don't add liquid paraffin to the diet of a furball-collecting cat permanently as it will reduce its absorption of some vitamins.

Abdominal problems

Besides containing important organs which can succumb to disease, the abdominal cavity itself can become infected.

Peritonitis

The lining of the abdominal cavity and the covering of the contained organs is known as the peritoneum. This can become inflamed for several reasons: □ infection gains entrance via a rupture in the abdominal wall or intestines □ infection spreads from other abdominal organs □ the presence of tumours □ germs arrive through the blood or lymphatic system from other places in the cat's body.

What are the signs?

The signs include: □ persistent pain in the abdomen □ the animal sits in a "tucked-up" posture □ it complains bitterly when handled □ vomiting □ diarrhoea or constipation □ fever □ severe loss of condition □ severe loss of appetite.

What is the treatment?

Prompt veterinary attention is essential. Diagnosis of the cause may involve blood tests, bacteriological examinations and, perhaps, an exploratory operation. Drugs are used to combat infections, and reduce the chances of internal adhesions forming which would affect the abdominal organs.

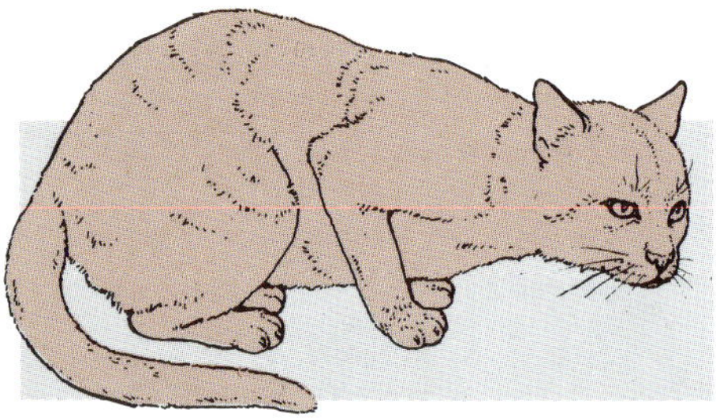

The tucked-up posture
A cat with abdominal pain due to peritonitis may assume this characteristic stance.

Feline Infectious Peritonitis

This particular infection of the cat's abdominal cavity is caused by a virus, and mainly attacks cats under three years of age as older cats generally have a natural immunity. FIP spreads rapidly by direct contact, and is consequently more of a risk in large groups of cats, as at a cattery. The germ can't live long outside the feline body, and is quite sensitive to ordinary disinfectants. However, once inside the cat as well as affecting the peritoneum it attacks several organs including the liver, kidneys and brain. The outlook for an infected cat is almost always bad, and most die after a few weeks of illness.

What are the signs?

Signs vary, but often include: □ fever □ chronic loss of weight and condition □ dropsical swelling of the abdomen □ vomiting □ diarrhoea. Also but less frequently: □ jaundice □ respiratory signs □ abnormalities in the nervous system.

What is the treatment?

Unfortunately, there isn't a vaccine available yet to protect cats against this disease. Treatment consists of combatting dehydration by replacing fluids, giving vitamin and hormone supplements, draining off fluid and fighting secondary infections with antibiotics.

You can play your part by keeping your cat warm and giving plenty of liquids (see p. 88).

Nutritional problems

Dietary problems shouldn't occur if your cat is given a good-quality, well-balanced menu (see pp. 28-9).

Obesity

Cats shouldn't weigh more than eight kg ; persistent overfeeding will result in gross obesity which will put strain on the heart, liver and joints.

Excess fats in the diet

Cats need a high percentage of fat in their diet, particularly as they get older. But too much fatty fish or fish oil can produce heart and fat tissue disease. The signs include: ☐ dullness ☐ stiffness ☐ soreness on being handled ☐ circulatory abnormalities ☐ fever. Vitamin E is used for treatment.

Calcium deficiency

The most important mineral to a cat, calcium is essential for pregnant and nursing queens and growing kittens. In kittens, skeletal deformities can occur, and in adults brittle bones and lactation tatany (see p. 74) may result. Lean meat is low in calcium, so include milk, fish (with the bones), and balanced proprietary foods in your cat's diet. Treatment consists of calcium supplements or sterilized bone flour.

Deficiencies of other minerals

Many other minerals are essential to cats (see p. 28), but deficiencies rarely occur as sufficient quantities are obtained from meat and fish.

Because cats eat a high-protein diet, they require a relatively large amount of iodine. Signs are: ☐ sluggishness ☐ alopecia ☐ scurfy, dry skin ☐ infertility. Iodine has to be given very carefully to avoid overdosing. Season home-cooked food with iodized household salt or give proprietary multi-vitamin/trace element tablets.

Vitamin A deficiency

Cats on a purely lean meat diet are sometimes deficient in vitamin A. Signs include: ☐ infertility ☐ abortion ☐ poor condition ☐ bone, skin and eye disease. Feeding liver or cod liver oil corrects the problem. But don't give too much fish oil – an overdose can lead to bone disease.

Vitamin B deficiency

There are several vitamins in the B group, all of which are essential for the cat. Deficiency of vitamin B1 can occur if too much overprocessed food or raw fish is given. Signs include convulsions and strokes. Vitamin B6 can be destroyed by overprocessing, leading to weight loss, anaemia and convulsions. Commercial cat foods have extra B vitamins added. Treatment for deficiency involves B-complex injections, yeast or multi-B tablets.

Vitamin D deficiency

A shortage of vitamin D, leading to bone disease, is uncommon in cats, and is caused by a diet of purely lean meat. Treatment is vitamin injections, feeding cod liver oil and a balanced diet.

PREVENTING NUTRITIONAL PROBLEMS

- Feed a well-balanced diet (see pp. 28-9)
- Lightly season food with salt or give multi-vitamin/trace element tablets designed for small animals
- Never overfeed (see p. 31)

Problems of the intestinal tract

The most common health problems encountered with the feline intestinal tract are diarrhoea and constipation.

Milk sensitivity diarrhoea
Chronic diarrhoea may be due to a deficiency of the milk-sugar-digesting enzyme, lactase, or to an allergy to milk protein.

What is the treatment?
In severe cases, the diet should be modified to exclude milk, milk products and most cereal products. Calcium supplements may be necessary. In mild cases, just dilute milk with water.

Enteritis and colitis
Inflammation of the small intestine alone is known as enteritis. Colitis is an inflammation of both the colon and rectum. Inflammation is caused by: □ bacterial or viral infections □ ingestion of irritant chemicals or poisons □ abdominal tumour □ chronic kidney disease □ parasites. Signs of intestinal inflammation may include fresh blood and mucus in the stools.

What is the treatment?
Get as much fluid as possible into the cat to combat the risk of dehydration. The vet will give antibiotics.

Feline Infectious Enteritis
Also known as *Feline Panleucopenia*, this highly contagious viral disease is resistant to many antiseptics, and can be transmitted by direct or indirect contact, even via fleas. With a 2–9 day incubation period, it invades the cells of the small intestine wall, the liver, spleen, bone marrow, some lymph nodes and, in unborn or newly born kittens, the brain. Cats may die within minutes of first showing signs of the disease. Less acute cases show signs that include: □ depression □ persistent vomiting □ diarrhoea □ rapid dehydration □ sitting in a typical "hunched-up" posture □ wailing pitifully when touched.

What is the treatment?
The vet will give fluids and stimulant drugs, also antibiotics to tackle any secondary bacterial infection. After seeing the vet, keep your sick cat warm and give it small, frequent helpings of warm glucose and water (see p. 88).

PREVENTING FELINE ENTERITIS

This fatal disease can be prevented by a vaccination given along with the "Cat Flu" vaccine (see p. 49) at 8-9 weeks of age. A second injection is given 3–4 weeks later, with boosters every 12 months. Dead vaccines are available, so a pregnant queen can be boosted to ensure high levels of antibodies in the colostrum and thus protect newly born kittens.

Constipation
Older cats, particularly longhaired, fastidious self-groomers, are the most likely to develop impaction of the large intestine and rectum.

What are the signs?
The cat may: □ strain hard to pass the faecal mass □ often show signs of pain □ gradually become dull □ crouch miserably □ show no interest in food or the world about it.

It is important to differentiate between straining caused by bowel impaction and straining due to urinary obstruction (see p. 70) as the two can resemble one another closely.

What is the treatment?
Start by giving liquid paraffin by mouth (see p. 88). If this doesn't work, the vet may give a softening enema. A disposable enema kit suitable for home use is available which your vet may prescribe, and instruct you on its use. Alternatively, you can give docusate sodium tablets by mouth; this chemical softens and draws water into hardened, impacted faeces.

If these measures fail, the vet will anaesthesize the cat and break up the mass directly. In a few cases, an operation may be necessary.

Obstruction of the rectum
The terminal portion of the intestinal tract is the most common site for a foreign body to jam, producing pain on defecation, irritation, constipation and sometimes straining.

What is the treatment?
Grease the anus gently with salad oil or liquid paraffin, or, if there is room, insert a glycerine suppository. If the obstruction doesn't clear as a result, consult the vet, who will remove it under anaesthetic. *Never* pull at any thread protruding from a cat's anus – it may run around bends in the intestinal canal, and you could easily lacerate the delicate lining. In such a case, consult the vet immediately.

Rectal prolapse
Persistent diarrhoea and straining may result in a short length of bowel turning inside out and protruding from the anus. Once out, this prolapse acts as an irritant, giving rise to more straining and, often, more prolapse.

PREVENTING INTESTINAL PROBLEMS

- Don't feed chicken bones
- Don't let the cat hunt and eat any wild food
- Groom the cat regularly to reduce loose hair
- Add a bulk-acting laxative as directed to the cat's diet

What is the treatment?
If your cat has a prolapse you *must* seek urgent veterinary attention. Before you see the vet, clean the exposed rectum with warm water on cotton swabs, then grease it liberally with liquid paraffin. The vet will push the prolapse back into place under anaesthetic and insert retaining sutures. Whatever caused the problem – often chronic diarrhoea – must be treated concurrently.

Anal irritation
In cats, irritation is usually due to the presence of wriggling tapeworm segments or matted hair following diarrhoea. Matted hair provides perfect conditions for the development of wet dermatitis (skin inflammation accompanied by a discharge), the moisture from which may attract blowflies to lay their eggs which hatch into maggots. An affected cat may turn round to spit at its tail, hold its tail pulled beneath it or make sudden little forward dashes.

What is the treatment?
Clip away all long, matted hair. Then wash the area with soap and water, rinse and dry it. Apply a human nappy cream. Where infection is present, an antibiotic ointment may be prescribed by the vet. If necessary, lightly dust with a proprietary powder (available from the vet) to kill maggots.

Problems with internal parasites

Found in virtually any of the cat's tissues, including the eye, lung and heart, the most common feline parasites are worms, and the most important group of these parasites are those which infect the gastro-intestinal tract: roundworms, tapeworms and flukes.

Roundworms
Two kinds of roundworms of the *Ascarid* family are commonly found in cats: *Toxocara* and *Toxascaris*. They don't suck blood, but feed on the digesting food in the cat's intestinal canal. Eggs are laid which pass out in the stools, and are then eaten by another cat, either directly, or after passing through mice, rats or beetles. Larval worms can penetrate the placenta to infest the foetus in the womb, and they are sometimes present in the mother's milk. Once in a kitten's body, the worms migrate through liver, heart and lungs to the intestine. Kittens are thus much more seriously affected than adults, and may develop: □ either diarrhoea or constipation □ anaemia □ pot-bellies □ poor condition.

Whipworms and threadworms
Smaller than *Ascarids*, these parasites are rarer in cats. Like roundworms, they have a direct lifecycle, the eggs and larvae requiring no intermediate host. The threadworm larvae inhabit the small intestine, where they burrow into the wall and may cause haemorrhages, whilst whipworms prefer the large intestine. Both parasites cause signs including: □ diarrhoea □ loss of weight □ anaemia.

Hookworms
These serious blood-sucking worms are more common in the U.S. than the U.K. They enter their host via the mouth or by burrowing through the skin, and then migrate to the small intestine. And they can pass to unborn kittens via the placenta. These worms produce signs of: □ diarrhoea (often blood-streaked) □ weakness □ anaemia.

Tapeworms
Not as dangerous as roundworms or flukes, tapeworms live in the small and large intestine and share the cat's

COMMON PARASITES

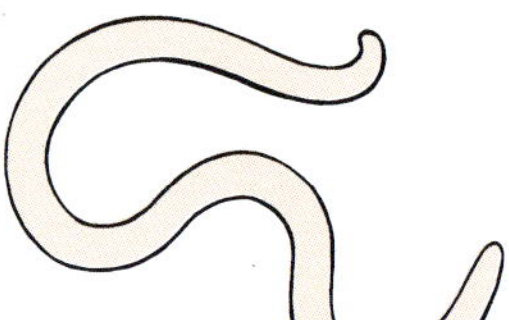

Roundworms
These large, creamy coloured worms are found in the cat's intestinal canal.

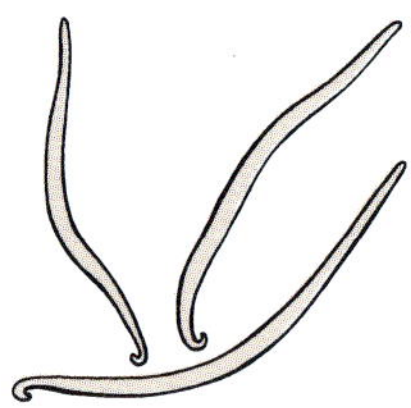

Hookworms
Named for their hook-shaped head, these blood-sucking worms live in the small intestine.

Tapeworms
These flat intestinal worms don't suck blood, instead they share the cat's food.

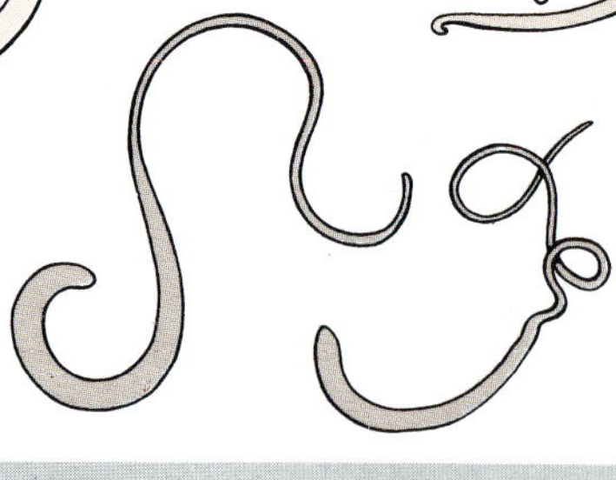

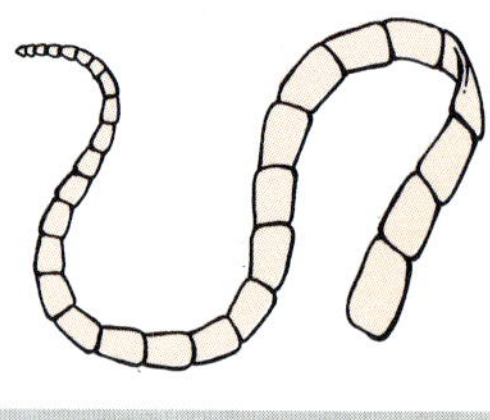

Whipworms
These tiny, thin, blood-sucking worms live in the cat's large intestine.

digesting food without sucking blood. Their presence may cause irritation and flatulence, but little else. When segments are passed through the anus they can cause irritation (see p. 65). The tiny, round eggs also pass out of the cat's anus, and these "rice grains" stuck to a cat's rear end are often the only sign of a tapeworm infestation. Once they have left the cat, the tapeworm's eggs must be eaten by an intermediate host such as a mouse or flea (one common U.S. tapeworm has *two* intermediate hosts, first a tiny crustacean, and then a fish). In this host's body they develop into a larval stage. Only when the intermediate host has been eaten by another cat will the larva be able to develop into another adult tapeworm.

Flukes

Found in the small intestine, pancreas and bile ducts, though rare in the U.K., flukes are fairly common in Asia, Europe and Canada. The intermediate hosts are a snail and a freshwater fish. Signs are: ☐ digestive upsets ☐ jaundice ☐ diarrhoea ☐ anaemia.

Other parasites

Cats can be infested with microscopic *Protozoa* parasites: *Amoeba*, *Trichomonas*, *Coccidia* and *Giardia*. All of these may produce diarrhoea and other gastro-intestinal signs, but are uncommon as causes of disease.

More important is *Toxoplasma*, which can invade various tissues of the cat's body, including the intestine, and is generally contracted through eating raw meat. Acute attacks, with signs that are easily confused with other diseases, may occur; these can be fatal. Chronic cases also exist. A common sign in both forms is diarrhoea. The cat sheds the parasites in its stools, and these can be passed on to humans. Although this disease is rare, it is a risk to pregnant women, who may pass it on to their unborn baby.

What is the treatment for parasites?

Ask your vet for advice on safe, effective deworming drugs. In most cases, your vet will recommend worming only healthy cats, unless the worms themselves are the cause of illness. It is generally advisable to worm queens before they become pregnant, and they can be safely treated when pregnant too. Two doses of worming drugs are usually given, with the second dose intended to catch immature parasites.

PREVENTING TOXOPLASMOSIS AFFECTING HUMANS

Careful hygienic precautions are important:

- Use disinfectant to clean the litter tray and surrounding area
- Change the litter daily
- Wear rubber gloves when handling litter (essential if you are pregnant)
- Cook all food for your cat thoroughly
- Keep children's sandpits covered
- Wear gardening gloves to avoid contact with infected soil

PREVENTING PARASITIC INFESTATION

- Stop your cat eating wild life
- Groom it regularly and use anti-parasitic powders to keep it free of larvae-carrying fleas
- Change bedding regularly to avoid the conditions that attract skin-burrowing worms
- Dispose of litter by burning, deep-burial or placing it in the dustbin
- Regular worming against tapeworms every 4 months and roundworms every 6 months is advisable

Liver and pancreatic problems

The liver and pancreas are employed in the process of digesting and metabolizing food and are therefore very important to a cat's well-being.

Liver problems
This important organ can be damaged by: ☐ poisons ☐ parasites (e.g. flukes or migrating worms) ☐ direct infections (Toxoplasmosis) ☐ indirectly when other organs are affected (e.g. by fevers or Feline Infectious Peritonitis) ☐ malnutrition ☐ tumours ☐ physical trauma.

What are the signs?
The signs of liver malfunction vary, and can range from the very dramatic (the cat may even die suddenly) to the very mild, and include ☐ jaundice ☐ collapse ☐ coma ☐ vomiting ☐ diarrhoea or constipation ☐ changes in stool colour ☐ increased thirst ☐ excitation (due to accumulation of waste products in the brain) ☐ swollen abdomen (due to an accumulation of fluid) ☐ depression ☐ dullness.

What is the professional treatment?
Only a vet can diagnose liver disease, generally by blood, urine and fecal sample analysis. The treatment is likely to include vitamin B complex, liver extract, glucose and corticosteroid treatment to raise the blood sugar level, increase the liver function and protect the cells.

What is the home treatment?
You should keep your sick cat warm and provide it with plenty of liquids at all times. Glucose and water (see p. 88) is preferable. You should also give it low-fat, high-protein diet.

Acute inflammation of the pancreas
Occasionally, a cat's pancreas becomes severely inflamed. This is usually very serious, and the cat may well die within hours or a few days. The signs include: ☐ vomiting ☐ tenseness and pain in the abdomen ☐ fever ☐ shock ☐ collapse.

What is the treatment?
Veterinary treatment *must* be given very quickly. It may include an intravenous injection of fluids, analgesics and anti-inflammatory drugs. The outlook isn't generally very good.

Chronic inflammation of the pancreas
Long-term inflammation will damage the pancreas. In such cases, the output of enzymes needed for the digestion of food and absorption of fat is lowered.

What are the signs?
This condition produces changes in the stools, which become clay-coloured, pale and fatty. With its ability to digest food efficiently markedly reduced, the cat develops a prodigious appetite, but loses weight and condition.

What is the treatment?
Following laboratory tests on the stools to confirm the malfunctioning pancreas, treatment involves providing a low-fat diet and adding substitute pancreatic enzymes to the food.

Diabetes
Diabetes mellitus or sugar diabetes is fairly common in cats, particularly in older, fatter individuals. And there seems to be a tendency to diabetes in some feline breeding lines.

GIVING YOUR CAT AN INJECTION

If your cat suffers from diabetes or certain other ailments, daily injections may be necessary. In the case of a diabetic cat, these will be of insulin. Your vet will supply you with the bottles of insulin at varying strengths, and with disposable, sterile needles and syringes. Insulin injections should always be given first thing in the morning.

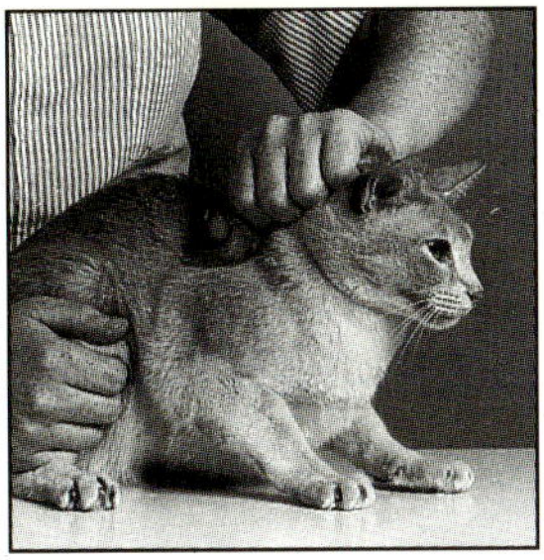

1 Test the urine to determine insulin needed, and prepare the syringe. Grasp your cat firmly by its scruff.

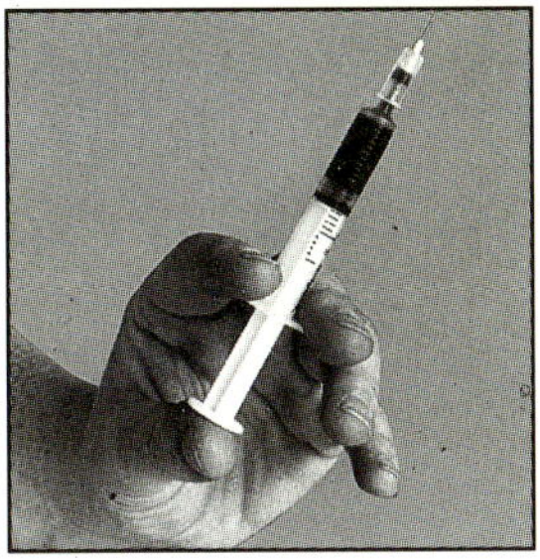

2 Point the syringe at the ceiling and press the plunger to force air out of it. Swab the site with alcohol on cotton wool.

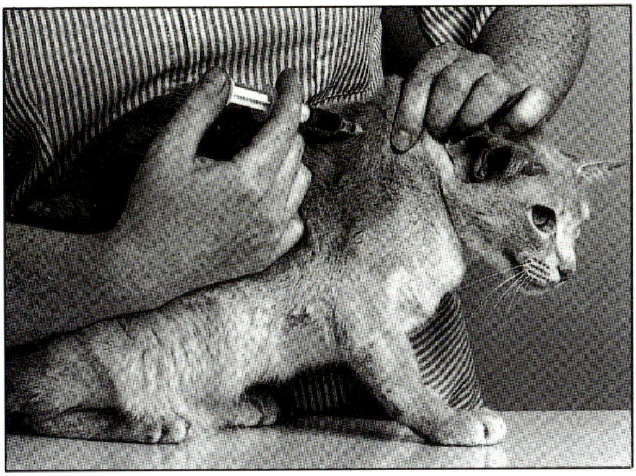

3 Push the needle through the skin into the layer of fat close to your "scruffing" hand. Don't worry about hurting your cat as most injections are painless, and the more relaxed you and your pet are, the easier it will be to administer the injection.

What are the signs?
The signs include: ☐ great thirst ☐ increased appetite ☐ a progressive loss of weight ☐ cataracts may develop in the eye ☐ in advanced cases, vomiting may occur. Diagnosis depends on the analysis of sugar levels in the blood and urine.

What is the treatment?
First, make sure that all carbohydrates, including any sugary treats, are eliminated from the diet. And cut out cat food that contains cereal such as barley. Your vet will instruct you how to give daily insulin injections – a relatively painless, simple procedure – and will also give you guidance on estimating dosage using the urine testing strips (these are dipped into a puddle of urine and change colour when sugar is present). The dosage may vary from time to time because of stress, illness or changes in diet.

DISORDERS OF THE URINARY TRACT

The kidneys, bladder and connecting passages are the route that various toxic wastes travel through to the outside world. Normally this waste takes the form of clear, yellow urine, but infection can affect its colour. The most common problem in this system is inflammation of the bladder and urethra. All urinary tract disorders are potentially serious, so a veterinary examination is essential.

INCONTINENCE

The natural place for a cat to urinate is at one of its territorial marks. With appropriate training, its litter tray soon becomes one of these. If your cat urinates elsewhere, clean the area scrupulously with a strong disinfectant to avoid a repetition of the soiling.

Things to look for

- Is the cat a new arrival? It may simply be nervous or unfamiliar with the location of the litter tray
- Is the cat an unneutered tom? If so, he may be marking his territory
- Has the cat's thirst increased? If so, it may have diabetes (see p. 68)
- Are there any other signs such as straining (see below), vomiting or diarrhoea? If so, the cat may have an infection

Possible causes

- Territorial marking
- Diabetes
- Bladder inflammation
- Urethral inflammation
- Damage to the bladder

Treatment

If your cat is a tom and is spraying, either arrange to have him neutered, or build a tom's run and keep him out of the house. If your cat isn't a tom and there are no other signs, give it a 250 mg hexamine tablet 2-3 times a day.

Don't restrict the supply of liquids available to your cat. Don't rub your cat's nose in the urine – this encourages it to re-use the spot as it becomes a territorial mark.

Urgency

✚ If there are no other signs, consult a vet as soon as convenient

✚✚✚ If there are other signs (such as straining, increased thirst, vomiting or diarrhoea) don't delay – consult a vet immediately.

STRAINING

If the cat appears to be straining (see the diagram opposite) and it isn't constipated (see p. 58), then it probably has a urinary blockage.

Things to look for

- Has the cat passed any faeces in the last 24 hours? If not, it may be constipated or have an intestinal blockage (see p. 64)
- Is the cat passing urine normally? If not, there is a possibility of a blockage
- Does the cat seem to be in pain? It may have a urinary infection
- Is the cat a queen due to go into labour? If she is, her labour contractions may be starting

Possible causes

- Constipation
- Intestinal blockage
- Cystitis
- Urinary "stones"
- Onset of labour

Treatment

There is little you can do before the vet's examination.

Urgency

✚✚✚ Don't delay – consult a vet immediately.

Problems of the urinary tract

Problems in this system are generally caused by infections. Kidney disorders are rare, but inflammation of the feline urinary tract is quite common. If you suspect a urinary problem, contact the vet immediately.

Acute kidney problems

Nephritis, or acute kidney infection, doesn't occur very often. Signs are: ☐ vomiting (may be blood-tinged) ☐ thirst ☐ inflammation of the mouth (often with difficulty in swallowing) ☐ severe dullness ☐ convulsions ☐ coma.

What is the treatment?

If the cause is a poison, the vet will try to get rid of the toxin. And in all cases, fluids are given to combat dehydration.

Chronic kidney problems

Old cats frequently show signs of chronic disease, starting with: ☐ great thirst ☐ increased urinary output ☐ loss of weight and condition. In advanced cases more signs develop: ☐ uraemia (retention of waste products in the blood) ☐ vomiting ☐ bad breath ☐ a sore, ulcerated mouth ☐ anaemia ☐ dehydration. In terminal cases death is preceded by: ☐ vomiting of blood ☐ convulsions ☐ coma.

What is the treatment?

Destroyed kidney tissue can't be replaced, so the load on the remaining kidney must be kept to a minimum. Give your cat a good-quality low-protein, high-carbohydrate diet: glucose, honey and sugar are useful energy sources. The vet may prescribe fluid injections, vitamin supplements, and suitable drugs.

Straining
A cat with a urinary blockage will crouch uncomfortably over the litter tray.

The bladder and urethra

At first, a cat with urinary trouble will strain to pass a little bloodstained urine. In more advanced cases this straining may be fruitless, the cat crouches in an awkward position (see above) and develops a distended abdomen. Do *not* squeeze the tummy – this is painful for the cat and may even burst its bladder. Most often found in neutered males, this condition is due to a gritty sludge in the urine blocking the passage. Causes are: ☐ too-early neutering ☐ low fluid intake ☐ dry foods ☐ old age ☐ obesity ☐ lack of exercise.

What is the treatment?

A blocked urethra needs immediate veterinary attention – the vet will free the blockage under anaesthetic.

PREVENTING URINARY BLOCKAGE

- Don't have males neutered until they are at least nine months old
- Provide plenty of water to drink
- Don't give too much dried food
- Add a little salt to your cat's meals to encourage it to drink

REPRODUCTIVE DISORDERS

This section is mostly concerned with problems of the female cat's reproductive tract as there are no special problems of the male feline genitalia. The most common condition in males is a bite wound inflicted by another tom, which should be treated like other wounds (see p. 93). If the injury is extensive or infected, consult the vet.

SIGNS OF PREGNANCY

- Reddening nipples – this is known as "pinking-up"
- Gradual weight gain – 1–2 kgs, depending on the number of kittens
- Swollen abdomen (*Don't* prod the abdomen to feel the foetuses – you could cause serious damage)

MISCARRIAGE

Premature onset of labour is uncommon in the cat. However, if a pregnant queen begins straining and the birth isn't due, suspect an imminent miscarriage.

Things to look for
- Is there blood or other discharge at the vulva?
- Are there any other signs of illness such as vomiting or diarrhoea? She may have an infection which has induced a premature birth
- Are you sure that she isn't going into labour at the normal time (nine weeks after season)?

Possible causes
- Accident
- Infection
- Foetal abnormality

Treatment
Keep the cat in a quiet place until the vet arrives.

Urgency
✚✚✚ If you are sure that the labour is premature, don't delay – contact the vet immediately. If in doubt, wait three hours, then contact the vet if no kittens have been born.

INFERTILITY

The failure of your queen to produce kittens may be the result of an unsuccessful mating or a physical defect in either her or the tom concerned. If the mating was concluded normally, the most likely cause is an infection in the queen's reproductive system.

Things to look for
- Has your cat been in an accident? If so, she may have had an early undetected miscarriage
- Is your queen exhibiting any signs of sickness or poor condition?
- Have her heat periods been regular? Frequent or permanent oestrus is a sign of ovarian cysts
- Did the queen show the usual signs of pregnancy following mating? A false pregnancy may have developed

Possible causes
- Undetected miscarriage
- Uterine or vaginal infection
- Pyometra
- Ovarian cysts
- Congenital absence or abnormality of reproductive organs
- False pregnancy
- Blocked fallopian tubes
- Failure to ovulate

Treatment
There is little you can do before the vet's examination.

Urgency
✚✚✚ Don't delay – consult a vet immediately.

Problems in the queen

Disorders of the female cat's reproductive tract won't affect a neutered cat. However, if you have an unneutered female (queen) she may suffer from one of these problems.

Ovarian cysts
When ovarian follicles don't ripen, but instead enlarge into cysts and turn out large quantities of female sex hormone, this interferes with the normal sexual cycle. Signs include: ☐ infertility ☐ frequent or permanent heat periods ☐ loss of condition and weight ☐ nervousness ☐ a generally discontented temperament.

What is the treatment?
The vet may use hormones to encourage the cyst to ripen and dissolve, or if that is likely to be ineffective, operate to remove the ovaries. Occasionally, surgery doesn't solve the problem, however treatment with the male hormone, testosterone, generally helps such cases.

Metritis
Infection and inflammation of the uterus (womb) may follow a difficult birth, particularly in a debilitated or older queen, or where placental material has been retained, or where a dead kitten was born or removed by forceps or Caesarian section. Signs may include: ☐ dullness ☐ lack of appetite ☐ fever ☐ pain in the abdomen ☐ unpleasant, smelly, bloody or purulent vulval discharge ☐ excess thirst ☐ vomiting.

What is the treatment?
The vet will give antibiotic injections, and may use a hormone to shrink down the uterus. Where dehydration has become evident, fluid replacement is essential; provide your cat with nourishing liquids such as beef tea, honey-water and protein hydrolysate.

Pyometra
Although this term strictly means "pus in the womb", it is used in veterinary medicine to describe a hormonal condition that occurs in the uterus. Structural changes, probably due to ovarian cysts, lead to thickening of the uterine wall, and the development of microscopic cysts. Inflammation then develops, and the uterus eventually fills with a sticky, pus-like fluid. Signs include ☐ vulval discharge ☐ dullness ☐ enlargement of the abdomen ☐ thirst ☐ loss of appetite ☐ vomiting ☐ poor body condition. Treatment involves removal of uterus and ovaries.

Prolapse of the uterus
Occasionally, following a difficult birth, some or most of the uterus will prolapse through the vagina, presenting itself as a bulging, red mass. Once the delicate lining membrane is exposed, it can easily be damaged.

What is the treatment?
Urgent veterinary attention is required. While you wait, keep the prolapse clean and moist, sponging it with warm water on cotton wool. Apply liquid paraffin or petroleum jelly to it, and cover it with clean cloth. If attended to quickly, the vet may be able to replace the uterus under sedative or anaesthetic. If time has elapsed or the case is severe, an abdominal operation will be necessary to fix the uterus back into place.

TREATING MASTITIS

This problem is generally caused by kittens scrabbling at the breast as they suckle, producing shallow lacerations through which bacteria can enter. You can relieve the swelling by applying a saturated solution of magnesium sulphate and warm water several times a day.

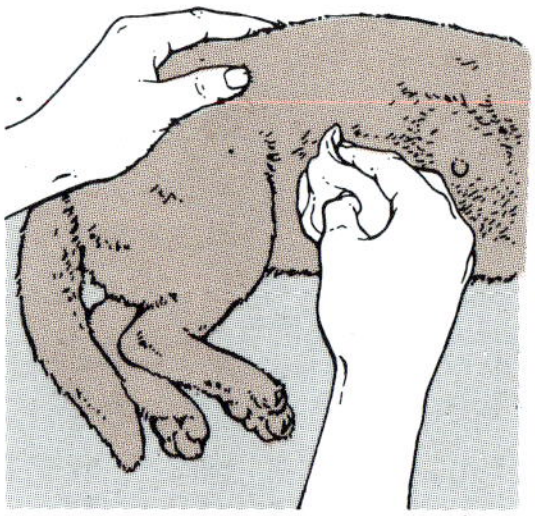

1 Swab the swollen gland with the magnesium sulphate solution on cotton wool.

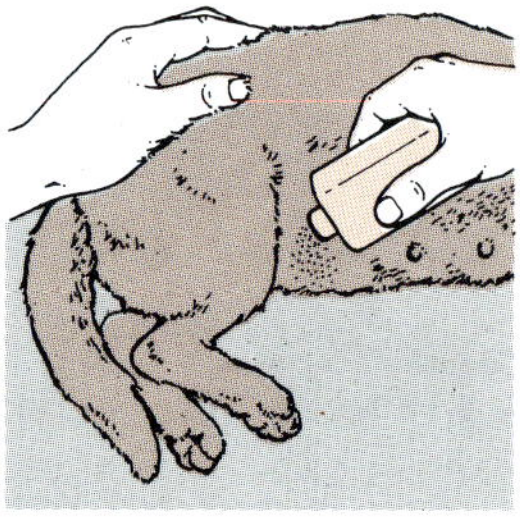

2 Dry the area gently and thoroughly, then lightly dust it with an antiseptic powder.

Post-partum haemorrhage

After a difficult labour a queen may sometimes haemorrhage from the uterus. In serious cases, shock, collapse and even death can result, so if this happens to your cat you *must* take her to the vet at once. Signs are: ☐ a flow of blood from the vagina ☐ constant licking of the vulva ☐ weakness ☐ pale mouth and eye membranes ☐ rapid, gasping breathing ☐ as shock sets in, the cat will feel cold and the pale membranes may turn blue.

What is the treatment?

Drugs will be administered by the vet to contract down the uterus and speed up clotting. If blood loss is severe, and the queen is in shock, a blood transfusion will be required, and the cat will probably be hospitalized for some time.

Mammary gland problems

Inflammation of a queen's mammary glands (mastitis) sometimes occurs during lactation. The signs are: ☐ swelling ☐ redness ☐ tenderness ☐ feverishness ☐ dullness ☐ disinterest in food ☐ refusing to let the kittens suckle.

Chronic mastitis, cysts and tumours frequently occur in older cats. Only a vet will be able to differentiate between them.

What is the treatment?

The vet will prescribe antibiotics. You can help by swabbing the swollen glands (see above). In the case of a tumour, surgery is performed at once.

Lactation tatany

Sometimes called eclampsia or "milk fever", this syndrome is caused by a fall in the calcium level in the blood, usually during lactation or, very rarely, during pregnancy. Signs vary, but include: ☐ muscular twitching ☐ tremors ☐ spasms ☐ staggering ☐ paralysis ☐ panting ☐ vomiting.

What is the treatment?

Urgent veterinary attention is essential; an injection of a calcium salt will be administered, and calcium supplements prescribed. This condition responds to treatment very quickly.

NERVOUS DISORDERS

The most common afflictions of the feline nervous system – the brain, spinal cord and the network of nerves radiating from them – are injuries caused by accidents.

STAGGERING GAIT

If your cat staggers, falls over, or has trouble standing upright, this may be due to a disorder of the nervous system.

Things to look for

- Has the cat ingested poison (see p. 94)?
- Has the cat been in an accident? It may have shock, or more seriously, cerebral or spinal damage
- Has it other signs such as vomiting or dilated pupils? It may have a severe disease

Possible causes

- Poisoning
- Shock
- Disease or injury to the nervous system
- Middle ear disease
- Muscular disease

Treatment

There is little you can do before the vet's examination.

Urgency

+++ Don't delay – consult a vet immediately.

TREMBLING

Trembling is rare in cats.

Things to look for

- Has the cat been in an accident? It may have shock
- Has the cat ingested poison (see p.94)?
- Has it signs of disease (see p. 37)?
- Are there any parasite droppings in the fur?

Possible causes

- Shock
- Poisoning
- Disease or injury to the nervous system
- Parasites

Treatment

If there is evidence of parasites, apply an anti-parasite powder or aerosol.

If the cause isn't parasites, there is little you can do before the vet's examination.

Urgency

+ Parasites may be treatable at home.

+++ In other cases, don't delay – consult a vet immediately.

PARALYSIS

If your cat can't move, the cause is either neurological damage or disease.

Things to look for

- Has the cat been in an accident? It may have a fracture or spinal injury
- Are the pupils dilated? It may have encephalitis
- Are its back limbs only affected? This indicates spinal disease or damage
- Has the cat ingested a poison (see p. 94)?

Possible causes

- Spinal injury or disease
- Fractured pelvis or leg
- Brain or bone disease
- Poisoning
- Tetanus

Treatment

There is little you can do before the examination.

Urgency

+++ Don't delay – consult a vet immediately.

Neurological problems

There are several health problems which can affect the brain and spinal cord of a cat, ranging from mild concussion following a fall to potentially fatal infections such as meningitis.

Meningitis

This uncommon disease affects the membranes covering the brain and spinal cord, and is usually caused by the spread of infection from some other parts of the body. Signs include: ☐ dullness ☐ depression ☐ loss of appetite ☐ fever ☐ convulsions ☐ dilated pupils. Swift veterinary attention is essential to save the cat's life. The vet will tap the spine with a hypodermic to take specimens of the cerebro-spinal fluid. Therapy consists of antibiotics and corticosteroids.

Encephalitis

Inflammation of the brain itself can be caused by: ☐ bacteria following septicaemia ☐ bacteria spreading from an infected middle or inner ear ☐ viruses such as Rabies ☐ fungi (yeasts, for example) ☐ protozoans *(Toxoplasma)* ☐ some poisons.

Signs can be very variable, and include: ☐ dullness ☐ fever ☐ dilated pupils ☐ staggering gait ☐ paralysis ☐ epilepsy ☐ coma. In many cases, the vet may find it difficult to pinpoint the cause. Where the cause is known, appropriate drugs are given. The cat should be confined to quiet, dimly lit surroundings.

Epilepsy

This is a disturbance in the functioning of the brain. The causes are often obscure, but may be related to parasites, a tumour or an injury.

What are the signs?

The principal signs are those of "fits": the cat keels over suddenly, and with little warning, frothing at the mouth, chattering its jaws and paddling frantically with its paws, oblivious to its surroundings. Faeces and urine are often passed involuntarily. After several minutes, the animal will quieten, lying still as if exhausted, and then shortly get to its feet as if nothing had happened.

What is the treatment?

For immediate action see *Convulsions* p. 92. If your cat has frequent attacks (more than once a month), consult the vet, who will administer an anti-epileptic drug.

Concussion

An accidental blow to the head stuns or bruises the brain, resulting in concussion. The animal is rendered unconscious for a period, after which it may show one or more signs of brain damage such as paralysis, a staggering gait or blindness. In most cases, such signs are temporary and last at most four or five days. Treatment may include drug and vitamin injections.

Myelitis and spinal cord damage

Damage to the spinal cord ranges from stunning and bruising to laceration or even severing, and generally occurs as a result of an accident. Myelitis is inflammation of the spinal cord, and can be caused by bacteria spreading from infected tissues nearby (often a septic bite wound in the back), viruses (for example, Rabies), parasites (such as wandering worm larvae and *Toxoplasma*) and poisons (for example, those produced by the tetanus or botulism germs and lead). Signs depend on the portion of the spinal cord affected, but include limb paralysis and back pain.

What is the treatment?
Treatment begins with identification of the cause and the use of specific drugs aimed at this. In some cases drainage of the spinal canal is necessary, and if paralysis is present, physiotherapy in the form of limb exercises is advised. Good nursing and control of secondary infections are essential, particularly where paralysis renders bowel and bladder control impossible. If after one month the paralysis hasn't shown *quite definite* signs of improvement, recovery isn't likely to occur at all. If improvement has been made, a full return to health will still take several months.

The Key-Gaskell syndrome
This mysterious disease has only been recognized recently, and the cause hasn't yet been identified. It is an odd ailment, usually affecting only one cat in a group, and is just as likely to strike a housebound cat as a free-ranging feline. The signs are: □ dullness □ loss of appetite □ vomiting and regurgitation of food □ constipation □ dilated pupils □ paralytic dilation of the gullet.

What is the treatment?
The vet will prescribe liquid paraffin as a laxative and give drugs which strengthen control of the nervous system. Unfortunately, the mortality rate is high at present (around 70 percent).

Local nerve paralysis
Sometimes a nerve supplying part of the body ceases to function and the area becomes paralyzed. Usually the result of an accident, this happens most frequently to the tail or a limb. Unable to control the appendage, the cat drags it about thus soiling it, and friction from the ground produces ulceration, and as the animal usually can't feel any pain, further damage can occur.

What is the treatment?
In cases where paralysis has existed for over a month without any perceptible sign of improvement despite treatment, it is best to have the leg or tail amputated (see below).

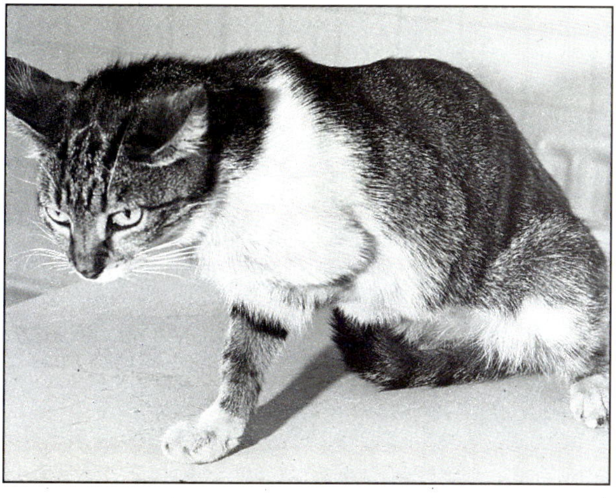

A feline amputee
Three-legged cats like the one shown here get around very well indeed, and recover rapidly from the operation. This treatment isn't in any way cruel, and the animal isn't turned into a cripple.

CIRCULATORY DISORDERS

Simple blood disorders such as anaemia are fairly common in cats, but heart conditions such as thrombosis are rare.

The heart

Several different kinds of heart problems are found in cats: kittens may be born with holes in the heart walls, infections such as septicaemia and feline influenza (see p. 49) can cause damage, and tumours, pneumonia and pleurisy (see p. 48) can also affect the heart. And as cats get older, the heart valves may get weaker or become blocked. Signs of heart disease include: ☐ a tendency to tire easily ☐ breathlessness or heavy breathing ☐ a lilac tinge to the gums ☐ coughing ☐ wheezing ☐ gasping and respiratory distress ☐ liver enlargement and malfunction ☐ intestinal upsets ☐ nervous signs.

What is the treatment?

The vet will listen to your cat's heart with a stethoscope, and may take an electrocardiogram, X-ray and/or blood samples in order to make the diagnosis. Treatment depends on the reason for the problem – certain drugs used on humans such as digitalis can be given to cats under strict veterinary supervision. Feline cardiac patients must be kept indoors, and taken for regular check-ups with the vet.

Iliac thrombosis

Thrombosis sometimes occurs in the main artery (the aorta). It is probably caused by a section of inflammatory tissue on a diseased heart valve breaking away, and being carried along by the blood stream until it jams in the aorta. Signs are dramatic and develop suddenly, they include: ☐ shock ☐ pain ☐ collapse ☐ partial or complete hind leg paralysis ☐ the hind legs feel *extremely* cold to the touch ☐ the femoral pulse (see p. 38) is absent in both hind legs.

What is the treatment?

Urgent surgery or drug treatment is necessary, and careful nursing is essential. Unfortunately, the recovery rate is low, and animals that do recover often suffer a second attack.

Heart worm

A round worm called *Dirofilaria immitis* is sometimes found in the right ventricle and pulmonary artery. This parasite affects cats in Southern Europe, the U.S., Far East and Australia. Larvae are transmitted to other animals by blood-sucking mosquitos or fleas. Signs aren't always produced, but where they are evident, they resemble those of heart disease.

If you live in a high-risk area control fleas and protect cats from mosquitos at night by keeping them indoors in mosquito-proof quarters with screened doors and windows.

What is the treatment?

Drugs are available which kill the worms, but the presence of the dead worms in the heart can in itself result in thrombosis or shock as the cat's body may react to the protein substances released by the dead parasites. However, larvae can be removed safely from the blood by drug treatment.

Feline Infectious Anaemia

This disease is caused by a parasite, *Haemobartonella felis*, which can infest feline red blood cells. It is probably transmitted by blood-sucking insects such as fleas and mosquitos. It may live in the red cells without causing much damage, but at times (for example, when a cat's resistance is lowered), it can destroy cells, resulting in anaemia. Signs are: □ dullness □ weakness □ loss of weight and condition □ pale eye and mouth membranes.

What is the treatment?
The vet will take blood samples to look for the parasite and estimate the degree of anaemia. FIA often occurs where there is a concurrent Feline Leukaemia condition. When a cat has both diseases the outlook is very poor, but where it exists alone the prognosis is good. Treatment consists of antibiotics, anti-anaemic therapy and, in severe cases, blood transfusion.

Anaemia
A reduction in number of circulating red blood cells and/or the amount of oxygen-carrying haemoglobin within those cells is known as anaemia. There are three main reasons why this happens:

1 The destruction of red cells by: □ parasites (as in FIA) □ a poison (for example, lead) □ a bacterial toxin □ an immunity reaction (as in an incompatible blood transfusion).

2 Loss of blood as a result of: □ an accident □ ingestion of an anti-coagulant chemical (such as the rodent poison, warfarin) □ a constantly bleeding ulcer, tumour or lesion □ the presence of blood-sucking parasites.

3 Reduced or abnormal production of new red blood cells in the bone marrow as a result of: □ a tumour □ a poison □ an acute infection □ a chronic septic condition □ chronic kidney disease □ tuberculosis □ deficiency of essential substances in the diet.

What are the signs?
The basic signs of anaemia are pale eye and mouth membranes. In advanced cases indications of "oxygen hunger" – weakness, breathlessness, fatigue and restlessness – may occur.

What is the treatment?
The vet will take blood samples to determine the cause and profundity of the condition. Anaemia isn't a disease in itself, merely a sign of an underlying illness. Therapy will include specific treatment for the cause, combined with iron supplements, drugs and, in some cases, a blood transfusion.

Leukaemia
This cancerous, controlled multiplication of white cells in the blood is fairly common in cats. Caused by a virus, Feline Leukaemia is contagious, and is spread by direct contact. It can't live long outside the cat's body, and is easily destroyed by disinfectants. Some cats are naturally resistant, whilst others develop immunity to it without showing any signs of illness. The unlucky remainder, once infected, develop signs which may include: □ anaemia □ weakness □ loss of weight □ vomiting □ diarrhoea □ respiratory problems.

What is the treatment?
There is no cure, and an infected cat should be put down to prevent the disease spreading to other animals. A blood test for the presence of the virus is available. Although cats that are positive to the test may not show signs of the disease, they may well be shedding the virus and thus are a source of infection. If they aren't euthanized, they *must* be isolated from other animals.

MUSCLE AND BONE DISORDERS

Diseases which affect the muscles, bones or joints are rare in cats, and the main health problems are due to injuries sustained in accidents or fights. Minor injuries such as sprains may be treatable at home, but if the cat seems to be in pain a veterinary examination is advisable.

Never give aspirin or use human linament; if you want to treat your cat before the vet's examination swab the area with an infusion of comfrey leaves in water.

TAILLESS CATS

Bone disorders are rare in cats. However, one breed, the Manx, suffers from a genetic abnormality so that every kitten is born without a tail or with only a rudimentary stump. The deformity is caused by an inherited gene, and is akin to the human spina bifida condition.

LIMPING

There are a wide range of reasons why a cat drags its leg or finds it difficult to put its full weight on it.

Things to look for

- Does the cat seem in pain if you touch the affected limb? This would indicate an injury or infection
- Is a single limb affected? If so, is it thicker than the other one? It may be fractured or sprained
- Is there any blood on the limb? The cat may have been in an accident
- Is there a swelling on the limb? A tumour may be the cause

Possible causes

- Bone infection
- Accidental injury
- Fracture
- Sprain
- Wound
- Tumour

Treatment

Apply first aid if necessary (see p. 93). Never give human or dog analgesics. Keep the cat indoors until the vet's examination.

Urgency

+++ Don't delay – consult a vet immediately.

SWOLLEN LEGS AND FEET

A sudden swelling of your cat's legs and/or feet is most likely to be the result of an infection.

Things to look for

- Has your cat been in a fight? A bite may have caused an infection
- Is a single limb affected? It may be fractured or have a tumour
- Does the cat look pot-bellied? Circulatory or kidney problems may have caused dropsy
- Does your pet seem stiff or have difficulty moving around, especially after a period of rest? It may have arthritis or another bone disease

Possible causes

- Bone infection
- Fracture
- Tumour
- Dropsy
- Arthritis

Treatment

Apply first aid if necessary (see p. 93). Keep the cat indoors until the vet's examination.

Urgency

+++ Don't delay – consult a vet immediately.

Problems with muscles, bones and joints

Always consult a vet if your cat shows signs of pain or stiffness, or if it is limping. *Never* give aspirin to a cat, even if it seems in pain, as this drug is toxic to cats.

Bone disease

Cats' bones lie fairly close to the surface of the body and are, in general, less protected by layers of soft tissue than those of humans or dogs. During a fight, the sharp teeth of a feline adversary can easily penetrate to the bone, and therefore limb or tail-bone infections are quite common. A pocket of infection, producing pus, is set up on or within the bone. If the marrow is involved a very serious infection known as osteomyelitis may develop. Wounds must therefore be treated before this serious infection can gain hold in the bone.

What is the treatment?
All bite wounds must receive veterinary attention – antibiotics will be prescribed to prevent the infection spreading to the bone. Treatment of osteomyelitis includes surgery to cut away areas of diseased bone.

Arthritis and joint disease

Inflammation of the feline joints is very rare, and chronic arthritis of the type suffered by humans or dogs seldom affects cats. However, occasionally an elderly cat may develop lameness due to the degeneration of a joint. If this happens to your cat, consult a vet who will prescribe anti-inflammatory drugs.

TREATING A SPRAIN

Sprains seldom occur in the lithe, light cat. When they do, signs are pain and diminished function of the affected part. Wrenched or crushed muscle fibres may be torn or bruised. Treat with hot and cold compresses and then support the affected part with a loosely wrapped bandage (see p. 93).

1 Immediately after the accident make a cold compress by soaking clean cotton wool or cloth in chilled water.

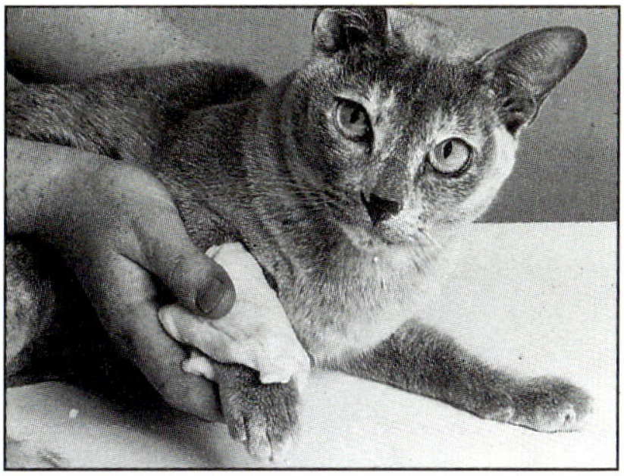

2 Apply a fresh cold compress every 30 minutes. After a few hours, change to a hot compress (water as hot as the back of your hand can bear).

DISORDERS OF THE SKIN AND COAT

The signs of skin disease in cats aren't specific to any one ailment: loss of hair, changes in the underlying skin, inflammation and irritation are common to a variety of skin conditions. Diagnosis requires professional examination, often aided by laboratory analysis of skin scrapings. Skin problems aren't always caused by disease or infestation – in some cases they are simply battle scars from fighting.

SEE ALSO:
Coat care see pp. 20-5.
Scratching see p. 45.

ECZEMA

There are many types of skin problem categorized under this name.

Things to look for
- Is the cat's diet broad? If not, it may have a vitamin deficiency
- Does the condition recur at regular intervals? If so, it may be an allergy
- Has it dry scaliness, redness, pimples, wet oozing, matted hair or hair loss? It may have a skin disease
- Are there any parasites such as fleas in the fur?
- Is the cat neutered? If so, it may have a hormone deficiency

Possible causes
- Nutritional problems
- Allergy
- Microbe attack
- Parasitic infection
- Hormone upset

Treatment
Clip matted hair, bathe in weak antiseptic, then dry. Apply cetrimide cream.

Clipping hair
Work carefully, making sure that you don't cut the skin.

Urgency
✚✚ Consult a vet as soon as convenient.

HAIR LOSS

If patches of your cat's hair fall out and it isn't the moulting season, a health problem is the likely cause.

Things to look for
- Is the skin reddened, broken, weeping or bumpy? If so, the cat may have fungal dermatitis
- Can you see insects or fine, black "coal dust" flea droppings in the coat?
- Is the cat's diet broad? If not, it may have a vitamin deficiency

Possible causes
- Fungal dermatitis
- Parasites
- Vitamin deficiency

Treatment
If the skin is affected, bathe it in weak disinfectant, then apply liquid paraffin. For parasites, use a proprietary powder. If necessary, correct the diet (see p. 63).

Urgency
✚✚ Consult a vet as soon as convenient.

Skin and coat problems

There are two main kinds of skin disease – parasitic and non-parasitic. Both are quite common in cats, and should be checked for at your regular grooming sessions.

Flea infestation

A cat can become infested with feline, dog or human fleas, the presence of which makes the cat scratch, twitch or lick itself frenziedly. Wherever fleas exist, what looks like coal dust can be found in the cat's coat. These particles are flea droppings. Reddish pimples with a darker, crumbly centre can develop, particularly along the spine as this area is sensitive to the protein in flea saliva. Fleas may carry tapeworm larvae, and can also spread certain viral diseases.

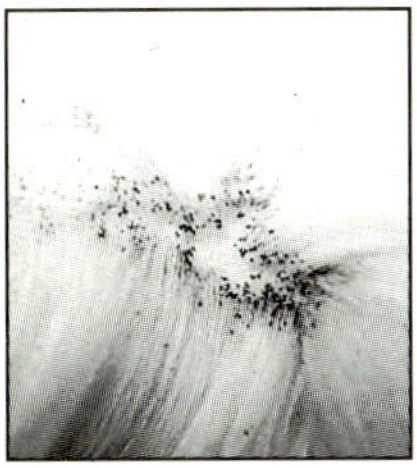

Signs of fleas *A black "coal-dust" powder found in a cat's fur is actually flea droppings. To check this, wipe them on a moist tissue — if they are droppings they will leave a dark red smudge (blood).*

Lice infestation

Two kinds of louse are found on cats: one sucking type, one biting type. The most common site is on the head, but they can make their home anywhere on the body. A heavily infested cat will be run-down and anaemic.

Tick infestation

Country-dwelling cats can pick up sheep ticks. These parasites suck blood, swelling up so that they resemble blackcurrants. You may mistake them for a tumour or a cyst. They don't move around as their mouth parts are buried securely in the cat's skin. For this reason, you mustn't pull them off as the mouthpart may be left behind, causing an abscess.

Mange mite infestation

These minute creatures burrow into a cat's skin, causing chronic inflammation, hair loss and irritation. The most common species is *Notoedres*, which affects the head and ear area, producing baldness, scurfiness and dermatitis.

Other mite infestation

During the autumn harvest mites or chiggers (*Trombicula autumnale*) can cause irritation and areas of dermatitis on a cat's skin. And the Fur mite

EXTERNAL CAT PARASITES

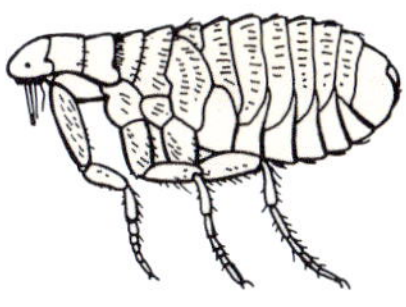

***Flea** (Ctenocephalides felis)* *Dark brown and the size of a pinhead, these insects can cause skin problems.*

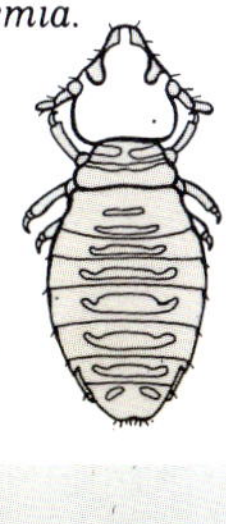

***Louse** (Felicola)* *This pinhead-size, grey creature can cause poor health and anaemia.*

***Sheep tick** (Ixodes)* *This large, round, blood-sucking parasite affects country cats and can cause anaemia.*

***Mange mite** (Notoedres)* *This mite can cause inflammation and hair loss.*

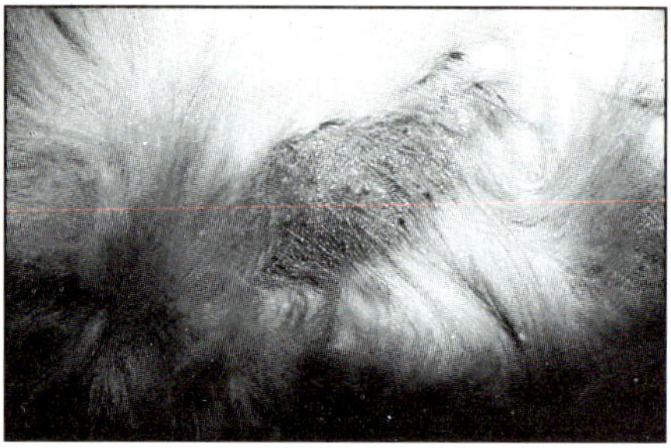

Signs of ringworm
This small, circular area with a bald centre and crusty outer edge is characteristic of ringworm, a common form of fungal dermatitis.

(which can affect humans as well as furry pets) causes excessive dandruff in the coat.

What is the treatment for infestation?
Seek your vet's advice on the best form of treatment for flea or mite infestation as there are many different types of anti-parasitic preparations on the market.

Remove ticks by applying a drop of chloroform or ether to them, waiting until the mouthparts relax, and then picking them off with tweezers. Once you have removed the tick, you should treat the cat with the appropriate anti-parasitic preparation.

PREVENTING HUMAN INFECTION

Humans can contract fungal dermatitis and some forms of mange mite, so take precautions to make sure the infection doesn't spread from the cat to the family. Burn all bedding and litter, and sterilize equipment such as boxes and utensils in a hot, cat-safe disinfectant.

Cat fleas and lice may bite you, but they can't live on you and therefore preventive precautions aren't necessary.

Fungal dermatitis

Caused by a fungus (*Microsporon* or *Trichophytes*), this skin problem takes the form of small, circular areas with bald centres and weeping or crusty outer edges or a general area of scaly, powdery skin.

After tests, the disease is treated either with an antibiotic given by mouth or an anti-fungal lotion or wash applied to the affected area.

Non-parasitic disease

Dermatitis and inflamed sores can be the result of: □ a bacterial infection □ a food allergy □ contact with irritant chemicals □ sunburn □ vitamin deficiencies □ hormonal problems.

What is the treatment?
Don't apply any ointment without veterinary advice – the cat may lick it off and suffer ill effects. Instead, clip away hair from the area, clean the skin with warm water and weak antiseptic and dry it carefully. Then contact the vet. If your cat licks or bites the area, fit an Elizabethan collar.

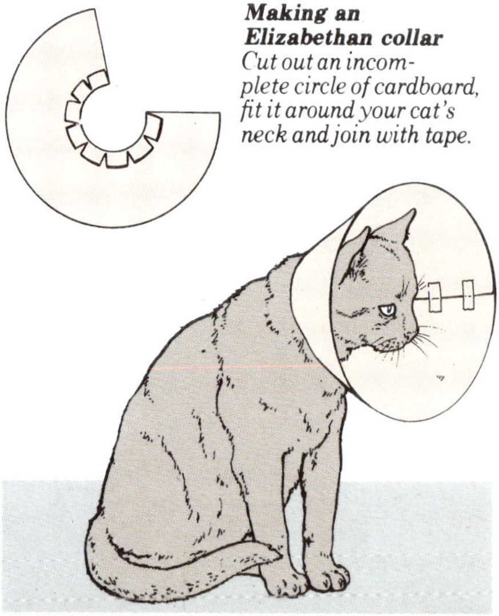

Making an Elizabethan collar
Cut out an incomplete circle of cardboard, fit it around your cat's neck and join with tape.

Keeping your cat healthy

With a little care, it is possible to reduce your cat's chances of becoming ill. There are four basic ways you can do this: keeping it out of danger, taking appropriate hygiene precautions, registering it with a vet, and having it vaccinated regularly.

Safety precautions

As a general principle, it is best not to let your pet wander far and wide, especially in an urban area – restrict it to your own garden, supervise its outdoor expeditions or train it to walk on a lead if possible. However, if it gets adequate exercise, I don't believe it is unhealthy or oppressive to keep a cat permanently indoors.

Hygiene precautions

For good feline health, hygiene is most important so keep your cat's bedding and feeding utensils scrupulously clean. Also, inspect its ears, eyes, nostrils, mouth, feet, fur, genitalia and anal area regularly to check that they are free from dirt, discharge and abnormalities (see p. 20).

Registering with a vet

As soon as you acquire a cat, register it with a vet. Ideally, you should choose one who specializes in the domestic cat or small animals. Such vets frequently have premises equipped with facilities for the most up-to-date medical and surgical techniques. A veterinary practice without such elaborate equipment may be capable of providing a high degree of medical care for cats, but it may refer complicated cases to other practices – ask to whom and where. Nevertheless, *all* vets are trained in feline diagnosis and treatment, and finding a vet who has a "feeling" for cats, who handles them with sympathy and interest, and who will explain the diagnoses clearly, is better than choosing a practice with advanced hardware and fancy surgical techniques.

Medical insurance

It is worth investigating a pet medical insurance scheme. This can ease the financial burden of unexpected disease and accidents.

Vaccinations

Make sure your cat receives preventive vaccinations against the major infectious diseases, and that it has regular booster doses (see pp. 49 and 64).

ELDERLY CATS

As cats age, they change physically, frequently becoming thinner, and their appetite often alters. These changes may be caused by failing liver and kidneys, conditions which, in the absence of other signs, are difficult for the vet to diagnose. All elderly cats should be examined by a vet every 3-4 months.

If your cat's appetite increases, give more food at each meal or more meals, and never deny increased thirst as this can be dangerous.

Many old cats suffer from bowel sluggishness and constipation. Others occasionally lose control of their bowels or bladder. If this becomes troublesome, ask your vet to check the cat. Adding bran, oily fish and, occasionally, liquid paraffin to the cat's diet may combat constipation.

Veterinary care

If your cat is unwell or injured, you will most likely have to take it to the vet's surgery or request a home visit. In all cases, telephone first and follow the vet's advice. In most instances, it is best to take your pet to the vet's, but for mini-epidemics among more than one cat in a household, difficulties while giving birth, if a badly injured cat is in an awkward spot, or if you are infirm and can't arrange transport, the vet may make a house call. You should withhold food and water before the examination in case an anaesthetic is needed.

The vet's examination

In the consulting room, the vet will ask for details of your pet's problem, and its past medical history. (If you have seen the vet previously your pet's medical record will be on file.) Be clear, concise and objective in giving information, and don't anticipate the diagnosis.

MOVING A SICK CAT

If the cat is in pain or agitated, hold its scruff firmly with one hand, with the other under its hindquarters. Wrap it in a blanket and place it in a carrying basket (see p. 13). A calm cat can travel on someone's lap.

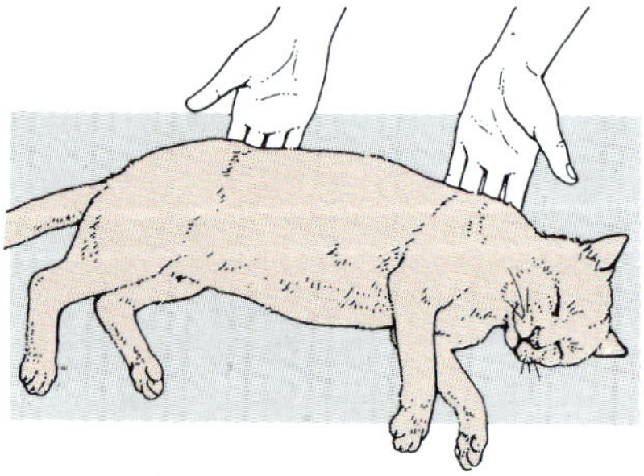

Moving a calm or unconscious cat
Gently turn the cat onto its side and lift it with two hands placed palms uppermost beneath the chest and the pelvis.

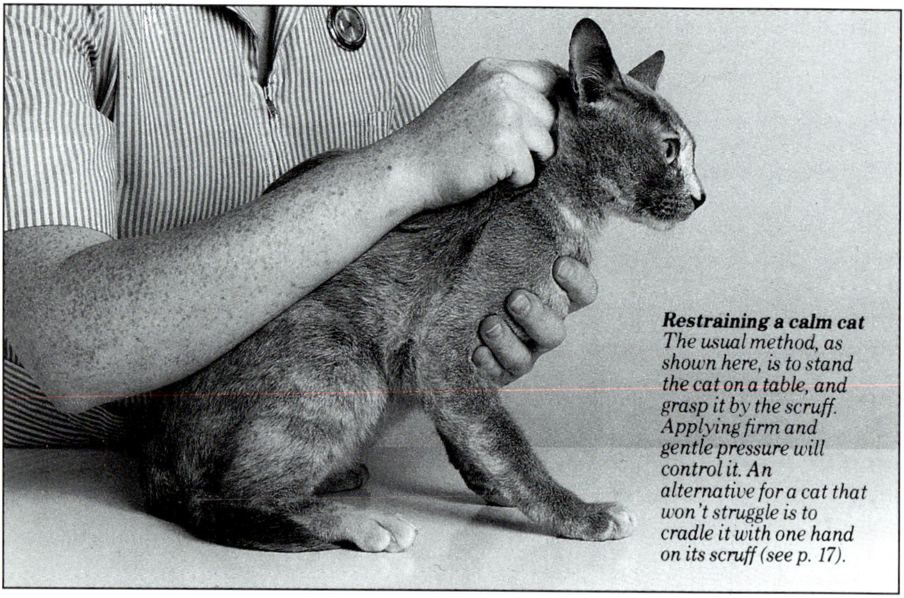

Restraining a calm cat
The usual method, as shown here, is to stand the cat on a table, and grasp it by the scruff. Applying firm and gentle pressure will control it. An alternative for a cat that won't struggle is to cradle it with one hand on its scruff (see p. 17).

EXAMINING AN AGITATED OR NERVOUS CAT

There are various ways of presenting an agitated cat for examination, depending on the form of the inspection and the state of the animal. In extreme cases, the vet may have to give it a tranquilizer. In all instances, the vet will handle the cat with your assistance or that of a veterinary nurse. You may find that wrapping your cat in a blanket (see below) for a while will calm it, and the vet will then be able to examine it unwrapped. Or the vet may prefer to immobilize the cat by holding its legs while carrying out the inspection.

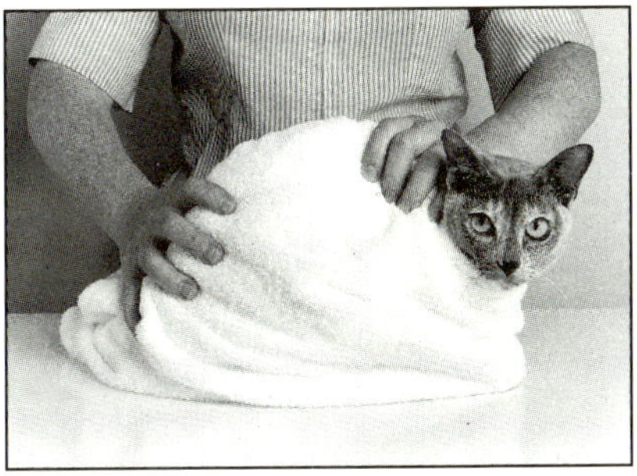

Restraining for a head examination
The cat is wrapped in a cloth or blanket, with only its head sticking out. This will enable the vet to inspect its eyes, ears, mouth or nose.

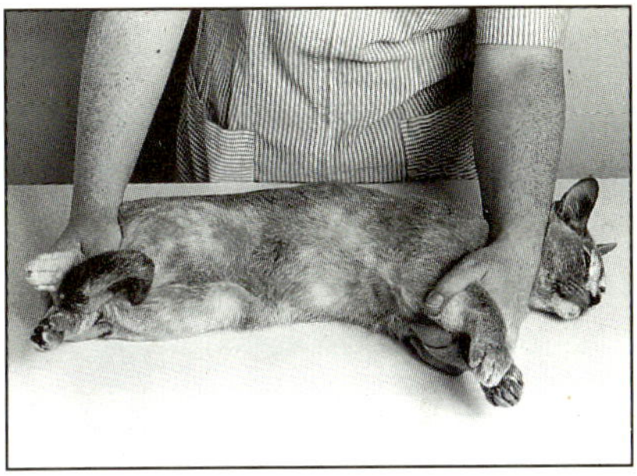

Preventing the cat from clawing
The cat is placed prone on the table with its legs held by the assistant. The animal is unharmed, but can't use its claws.

After the diagnosis
Your vet will tell you whether home nursing (see p. 88) will be possible, or whether your pet should be left at the surgery for hospitalization so that further diagnostic or therapeutic measures can be carried out. Some new developments in small-animal medicine are best performed "in hospital", where the staff can monitor your pet. In other cases, home care in familiar surroundings may be preferable.

Death

If you are fortunate, your cat will die in its sleep when its time comes. However, if a cat is in pain that isn't likely to be relieved, or if the animal is diseased and obviously unhappy, then as a humane owner, you will have to make a difficult decision. I feel it is irresponsible to deny the creature a dignified end.

Euthanasia
This merciful procedure is an extension of deep general anaesthesia. The vet injects an overdose of an anaesthetic either intravenously or into the chest. Rapid, painful poisons are never used, and the only pain is that of a needle prick. You may ask to watch the procedure, if you wish. Most vets can arrange cremation or burial for your pet, or you may prefer to bury it yourself or take it to a pet cemetery.

If your vet suggests that a post-mortem examination is of value, I recommend you agree as your pet won't feel anything, but may contribute to the advancement of pet health.

Home nursing

If your cat should become ill, you will need to provide it with a comfortable, hygienic rest area, and a nutritious, tempting diet. And you may have to administer drugs prescribed by the vet.

Providing a suitable "sick-room"
The main requirements of a sick cat are rest and warmth. It should be provided with a clean, heated, airy environment and snug, regularly changed bedding. Good draught-free ventilation is particularly important if your cat has a respiratory ailment. Warmth can be provided by background central heating or by a fan heater, infra-red lamp, hot water bottle or blankets. But take care when using infra-red lamps and hot water bottles, as they can cause burns if placed too close to a cat. Set up and turn on the lamp,wait a minute or two, then test the distance (usually a minimum of 60 cm) by placing your hand where the cat will lie. Hot water bottles are best wrapped in a cloth cover before being put in contact with the patient.

Don't under *any* circumstances allow a sick, convalescent or injured cat to go out of doors. It must remain under your round-the-clock control until it has completely recovered.

Feeding a sick cat
Loss of appetite is a common feature of many feline illnesses, but cats rarely die from starvation, even after many days without solid food. But dehydration caused by a drastic reduction in the fluid intake can be aggravated by vomiting and/or diarrhoea, and can kill a cat very quickly. You should therefore provide nourishing liquid food and, if necessary, spoonfeed your cat. Give it 1–3 tsp as often as possible.

SPOONFEEDING A CAT

Grasp it by the scruff, and twist your wrist so that the head is flexed backwards and the mouth opened. Then spoon in the liquid, drop by drop, letting it run down the tongue.

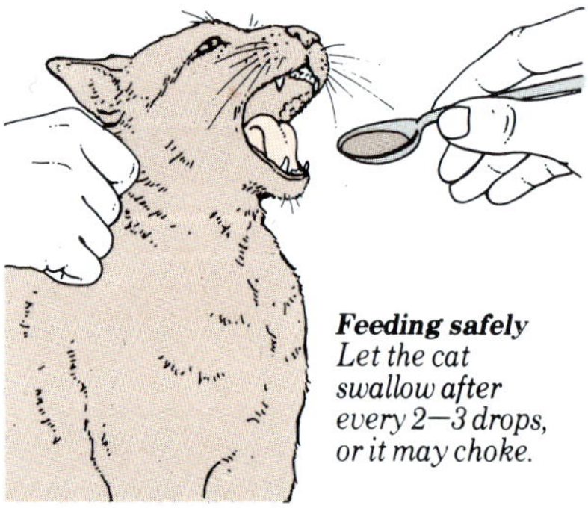

Feeding safely
Let the cat swallow after every 2–3 drops, or it may choke.

Invalid foods
Unless the vet advises giving a special diet, feed your pet a variety of tempting, high-value, tissue-building foods – those that are rich in protein, minerals and vitamins – and give energy-rich, easily digested items to provide calories.

Liquids
- Dilute glucose (2 tsp :1 cup of water)
- Dilute honey (2 tsp :1 cup of water)
- Beeftea
- Warmed, liquified calf's foot jelly
- Proprietary liquid invalid foods

Solids
- Fresh fish and shellfish
- Best quality minced meat
- Cheese and eggs
- Cooked poultry, lamb or pig's liver
- Meat- and fish-based baby foods
- Mashed potatoes and cooked rice

Administering drugs

You should be able to serve pills, tablets or liquid medicines yourself. However, if your cat requires an injection, the vet will give this, unless the cat is diabetic, when you will be instructed in the method (see p. 69).

Pills and tablets

Follow the instructions below. Don't crush the tablet and sprinkle the resulting powder onto the tongue as many drugs have an unpleasant or bitter taste which will cause the cat to produce copious, foamy saliva and to become agitated.

Liquid medicines

The easiest way of giving cats these is by spoonfeeding (see opposite). Very bitter liquids and some tablets crushed and mixed with water may produce salivation in the cat. Most cats can detect drugs mixed in their food and will refuse to eat.

Injections

For these, you may need to make regular, possibly daily, visits to the vet, but in some cases a continuous therapeutic action over several weeks can be obtained with a single injection.

Sick-room hygiene

During illness, it is especially important to continue with the regular hygiene, grooming and inspection of your pet (see p. 20). Also, disinfectants should be used to clean the "sick-room" area.

Warning: Many commonly used household disinfectants – the phenolic, coaltar and woodtar, hexachlorophene and iodine preparations – are dangerous for cats. Other disinfectants are safe for general use if diluted as indicated on the containers. These include cetrimide, quaternary ammonium compounds, and the safest and most effective, dodecine. To find out whether a disinfectant is suitable, study the list of ingredients on the label.

GIVING YOUR CAT A PILL OR TABLET

Generally two people are required, one to immobilize the cat by pressing it down firmly onto a flat surface with one hand on its scruff, while the other person acts as the "pill pusher". You can use your fingers, the blunt end of a pencil or a "pill gun" to push the pill further into the cat's mouth. Smearing the pill with butter may help its passage. Once you have pushed the pill down the cat's throat, close its mouth and stroke its throat until it swallows.

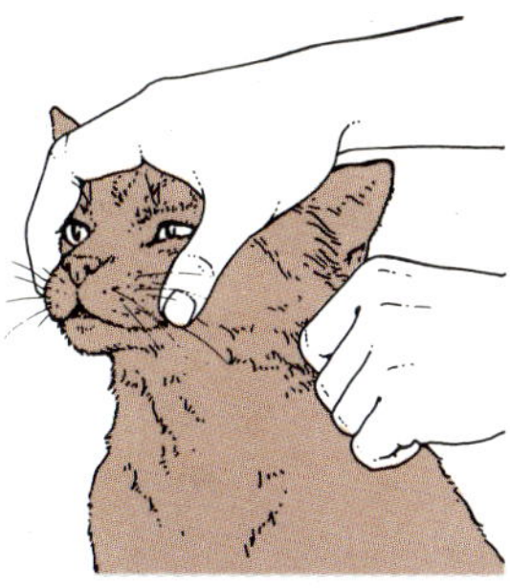

1 With forefinger and thumb, grasp the head from above where the jaws meet, and tip it back. Press finger and thumb in.

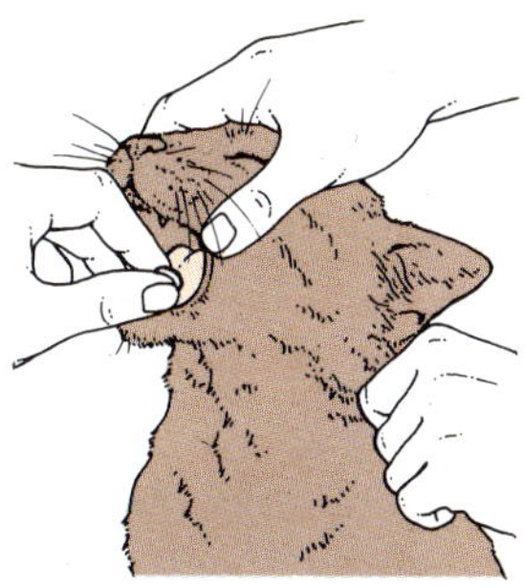

2 Push on the lower jaw with the other index finger. Drop the pill far back on the middle of the tongue. Push it quickly so it moves over the back of the tongue.

Collapse and accident

An injured or unconscious cat may need prompt first aid action – stopping bleeding, treating shock, clearing its airways and giving artificial respiration – in order to save its life. You should therefore familiarize yourself with the basic methods involved. If possible, get someone else to telephone the vet so that you can begin the emergency procedure straightaway.

SEE ALSO:
Taking the pulse see p. 38.
Wounds and burns see p. 93.
Restraining a cat see p. 86.
Convulsions see p. 92.

DO NOT:

- Don't move the animal unless it is in danger (if it is lying in the road, for example)
- Don't raise its head or prop it up because saliva, blood or vomit may run to the back of the throat and block the airway
- Don't give the animal anything – solid or liquid – by mouth, as the vet may wish to give an anaesthetic when he examines it

ACTION

1 Getting the cat out of danger If you have to move an injured cat slip a sheet under it and carry it like a hammock. You may need to restrain it first (see p. 86). Lay the cat down in a quiet, warm place and cover it with a blanket. Place a hot water bottle next to it. Make sure it isn't scalding – it is safest to wrap the bottle in a cloth. This will help to calm the shocked cat.

2 Check the pulse This can be felt on the inside of the cat's thigh, where the leg joins the body (see p. 38).

3 Check breathing If breathing is irregular or nonexistent: □ loosen the collar □ open the mouth □ pull the tongue forward □ remove any foreign body present (see p. 92) □ wipe away any saliva, blood or vomit □ give artificial respiration.

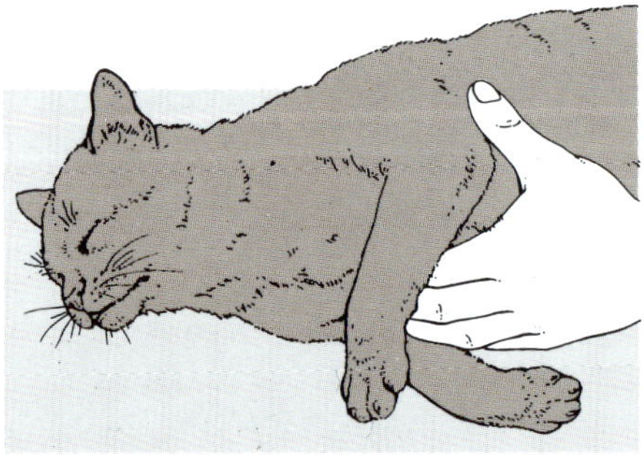

4 Check for heartbeat This can be felt by placing the fingertips on the lower part of the chest, just behind the front leg. Give heart massage if necessary – rub the area over the heart vigorously but carefully (it is easy to crush its ribs) with both hands. Also give artificial respiration (see opposite).

5 Treat bleeding Staunch any heavy blood flow (see p. 93).

6 Look for broken bones Give emergency treatment.

7 Treat shock Keep the cat warm with blankets or hot water bottles.

8 Contact the vet Arrange for an immediate examination.

Possible causes of collapse
□ Epileptic fit (see p. 92) □ Heart disease (see p. 78) □ Poisoning (see p. 94) □ Diabetes (see p. 68) □ Severe exposure □ Injury in an accident

A BASIC FIRST AID KIT

Keep a separate kit: **1** Safe disinfectant (p. 89) **2** Milk of magnesia **3** Human eye wash **4** Liquid paraffin **5** Antiseptic cream **6** Antiseptic wash **7** Round-ended scissors **8** Tweezers **9** Stubby thermometer **10** 5 and 10 cm bandages **11** 5 cm adhesive dressing **12** Cotton wool **13** Cotton buds **14** Lint gauze **15** Plastic bags to cover foot dressings

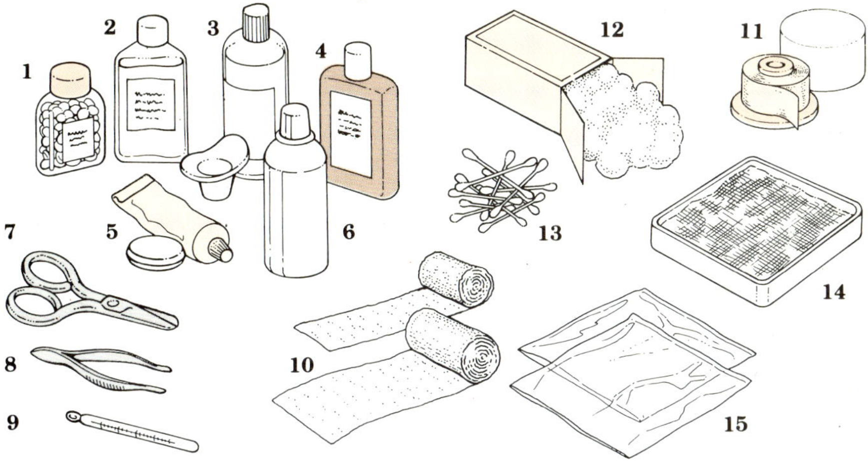

ARTIFICIAL RESPIRATION

Unless the cat is unconscious or there is a possibility that its back or hind legs are injured, it is best to start by swinging it (see p. 92). This will clear fluid and mucus from the airways. If this doesn't work, you will probably find the external method easiest. If the cat is unconscious or you suspect chest damage, the mouth-to-mouth method is best. With both methods, keep the cat horizontal during treatment.

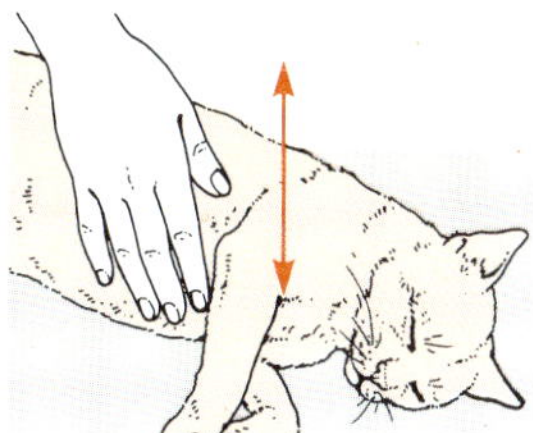

External method
Place both palms on the chest over the ribs and push down firmly to expel air from the lungs. Be careful not to press too firmly or you may damage the cat's ribs. Release pressure straightaway so that the chest expands and the lungs refill. Repeat at 5-second intervals.

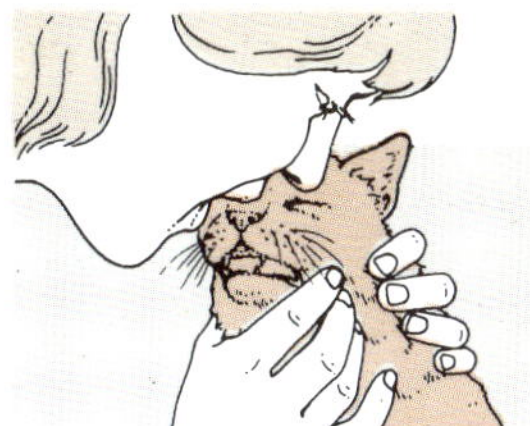

Mouth-to-mouth method
Check that the airway is clear, then apply your lips to the cat's nostrils and blow in air steadily for 3 seconds. Pause for 2 seconds, then repeat.

CONVULSIONS

Most fits, including epileptic types, start with uncharacteristic, bizarre behaviour which may include: □ Champing □ Chewing □ Foaming at the mouth □ Jerking of the limbs □ Incontinence □ Collapse. This is followed by loss of consciousness.

ACTION

1 Contact the vet immediately.

2 Make sure that the cat is in a safe place.

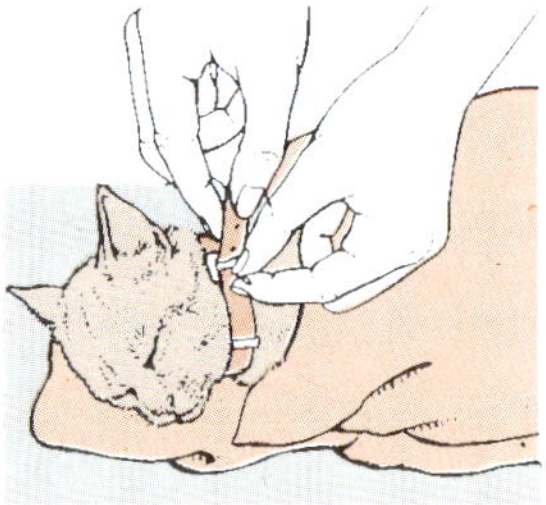

3 Leave the cat where it is, but try to make it as comfortable as possible by loosening its collar and covering it with a blanket to keep it warm. Once you have done this, try to avoid touching it until the fit is over.

4 Reduce external stimuli (dim the room lights, draw the curtains and turn off the radio or television).

5 The fit shouldn't last longer than five minutes. Once it is over, wipe the froth from the cat's mouth and clean up any urine and faeces.

6 Keep the animal indoors in a warm, quiet place until the vet arrives.

Foreign body in mouth
Grasping the cat's body firmly, open its mouth and push the lower jaw down with a pencil. Locate the object, using a torch if necessary, and remove it with fingers or fine pliers. If you can't dislodge the obstruction try the swinging method (right). Now contact the vet.

Foreign body in the eye
Don't allow the cat to paw at its eye. Grasping its body firmly, part the eyelid and examine the eye. If the foreign body is penetrating the surface *don't* attempt to remove it, go straight to the vet. If the object doesn't wash out, put 1–3 drops of olive oil in the eye. Contact the vet.

Foreign body in the nose
Don't try to remove the object. First apply a cold compress to soothe irritation and control bleeding. Now contact the vet.

Resuscitating a drowning cat
Pick it up by its back legs and whirl it round and round so that centrifugal force drives out the water blocking the airways.

Wounds and burns

The most common causes of wounds are bites or scratches from other cats. If you notice blood on your cat's coat and can't find the source, run your fingers through its coat to locate the wound.

ACTION

1. **Clean the area** Clip surrounding hair if necessary (see p. 82).
2. **Control any bleeding** Bandage the wound (see below).
3. **Treat shock** Keep the cat warm with blankets or a hot water bottle.
4. **Contact the vet** Arrange for an immediate examination.

TREATING BURNS

Burns are usually caused by hot liquid spilt on a cat. However, chemicals, extreme cold and electric current can also be causes. Apply cold water or ice to the site. (If the cause is a burning chemical, wash it off with copious amounts of water.) Then apply a greasy ointment such as petroleum jelly to the burn. Now contact the vet.

White cats sometimes suffer from sunburn to the ears. Ask your vet for a healing ointment, and keep your cat indoors in sunny weather.

BANDAGING

Use hospital-quality bandages, making a two-thirds overlap every turn, and keeping the degree of tightness even. When bandaging a limb, take the bandage down to envelop the foot. This avoids a "tourniquet" effect where the circulation in the lower leg is adversely affected by the bandage.

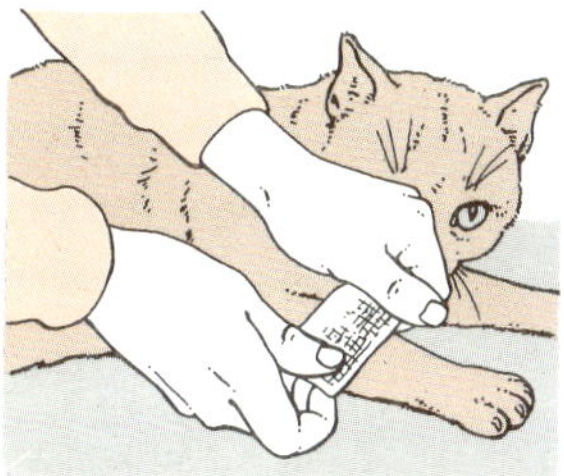

1 Cover the wound with a pad (at least 1 cm thick) of absorbent material.

2 Secure the pad with a crepe bandage fixed with a safety pin.

PRESSURE POINTS THAT CONTROL BLEEDING

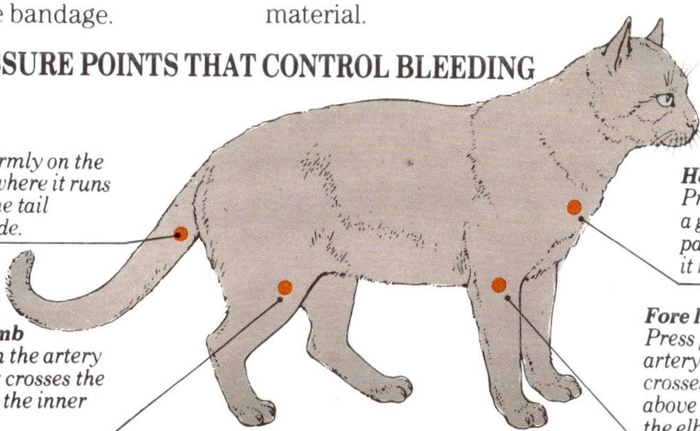

Poisons

Cats are at risk from a number of poisons, ingested in two main ways: first, if a cat's coat becomes contaminated with a chemical it will lick it off in an attempt to clean itself, and second its hunting lifestyle means that a cat may eat, unwittingly, poisons used to kill pests. Don't try to make an accurate diagnosis of the kind of poison from its effect – many different types produce similar signs.

ACTION

1 Contact the vet Arrange for an immediate examination.

2 Wash the cat at once Use human hair shampoo or even soap. Rinse it well, and dry it thoroughly.

3 Visit the vet If you suspect a particular chemical causant, bring a sample of it and its container with the cat.

Treatment
If indicated (see below), or on your vet's advice give an emetic to make the cat vomit, a demulcent to protect its stomach and intestines, or a laxative.
Emetics Suitable substances are: □ a pea-sized piece of sodium carbonate given as a tablet □ a very strong solution of salt in water □ mustard in water.
Demulcents Suitable substances are: □ milk □ raw egg white □ milk of magnesia □ olive oil.
Laxatives Suitable substances are: □ liquid paraffin □ magnesium sulphate.

COMMON POISONS

Type	Source	Visible signs	Emergency action
Arsenic	• Horticultural sprays • Rodent poisons	• Vomiting • Diarrhoea • Paralysis	• Wash coat • Emetic • Demulcent
Lead	• Paints	• Paralysis • Nervous signs	• Wait for vet
Phosphorus, Thallium	• Rodent poison	• Vomiting • Diarrhoea	• Emetic
Phenols, Cresols, Tar products, Turpentine	• Tar • Wood preservative	• Burnt mouth • Vomiting • Convulsions • Coma	• Wash coat • Demulcents, particularly milk
Aspirin		• Vomiting • Liver damage	• Emetic • Demulcent
Chlorinated hydrocarbons (DDT, Gamma BHC)	• Insecticides	• Nervousness • Salivation • Convulsions	• Wash coat • Wait for vet
Warfarin	• Rodent poison	• Stiffness • Diarrhoea • Haemorrhages	• Wait for vet

Index

Acknowledgements

Author's Acknowledgements
I would like to thank the Dorling Kindersley team, particularly Judith More and Carole Ash, for their expertise, enthusiasm and many kindnesses. Thanks are also due to Diane Wilkins who typed the manuscript and whose family stoically endured my dictation tapes, to my daughter Lindsey for much help and to the members of my practice for wise advice. Lastly, I must mention my parents - it was as a result of their encouragement when I was a small boy that I became a veterinary surgeon.

Dorling Kindersley would like to thank:
Peter Scott, Iona McGlashan, Lesley Davy, Bruce Fogle, Jenny Berry, Maxine Clark, Mr and Mrs Ash, Karen Fletcher, Neil Cousins, Richard Warner, Sal Marsh, Richard Ollet, Mr Klauf Defsauer, Spud, Tiger, Robin, Daisy, and Unigraph.

Illustrators
Coral Mula, Chris Forsey, John Woodcock, David Ashby.

Photography
Paddy Cutts or Karen Norquay except for:
Animal Health Trust: pp. 54, 55 c
Animals Unlimited/Paddy Cutts: p. 30
Stephen Dalton/NHPA: p. 33
Farming Press Ltd.: pp. 55 l, 77, 92
Tony Stone Photolibrary - London: pp. 1, 2, 26
University of Glasgow Veterinary School: pp. 55 r, 83, 84
Sam Zarember/Image Bank: p.7, cover.

Typesetting by Gedset, Cheltenham
Reproduction by fotolito CLG, Verona